SO AMAZING, SO DIVINE

So Amazing, So Divine

A GUIDE *to* LIVING PRAYER

Isaac Watts

COMMENTARY *by* HAL M. HELMS

PARACLETE PRESS
BREWSTER, MASSACHUSETTS

Scripture quotations found in the commentaries are taken from the Revised Standard Version of the Bible, copyright 1946, 1952, 1971 by the Division of Christian Education of the National Council of the Churches of Christ in the USA. Used by permission.

All other Scripture quotations are taken from the King James Version of the Bible.

Library of Congress Cataloging-in-Publication Data

    Watts, Isaac, 1674–1748
    So amazing, so divine : a guide to living prayer / by Isaac Watts : commentary by Hal M. Helms.
          p. cm.
     ISBN 1-55725-182-7 (pbk.)
     1. Prayer—Christianity—Early works to 1800. I. Helms, Hal McElwaine. II. Title.
    BV215.W375   1997
    248.3'2—dc21   97-21466
                                                      CIP

10 9 8 7 6 5 4 3 2

Published by Paraclete Press
Brewster, Massachusetts
Printed in the United States of America.

Introduction

In seminary in the 1950s, one professor who had spent most of his career as a pastor told us, "Make three books your primary resources: the Bible, the Book of Common Prayer, and the Hymnal." Since the student body was made up of what could be called "free churches," i.e., nonliturgical churches, the inclusion of the Book of Common Prayer might seem strange. But those of us who followed his advice found that reading and absorbing the prayers in that venerable book helped to shape and change our "free prayers" which we were obliged to offer in the pulpit each week.

Isaac Watts (1674–1746) was an Independent (Congregational) minister whose fame rests on his hymns and his paraphrases of the psalms. Lord Selborne said, "The Independents, as represented by Dr. Watts, have a just claim to be considered the real founders of modern English hymnody." James Montgomery, himself an able hymn writer, said of him, "Dr. Watts may almost be called the inventor of hymns in our language, for he so far departed from all precedent that few of his compositions resemble those of his forerunners. . . ." The great Dr. Samuel Johnson said of him, "Few men have left behind such purity of character or such monuments of laborious piety."

He was physically small and often plagued with illness. There were whole years when he was unable to minister from the pulpit, but his writings gave him an outlet for his concern that the free worship of the Independents not fall short in dignity and reverence to that of the Church of England.

Isaac Watts is speaking primarily to those who practice and believe in free prayer. His concern is that we as individuals, as well as the groups in which we pray aloud, will be spared from meaningless clichés, awkward expressions, and distorted petitions as we speak to the Majesty on high.

Today's praying, like today's language, tends to be much less formal than was the case in Dr. Watts's day. Not only has our language lost many of the words that were current in his day, but our way of expressing ourselves tends to be less discursive. What holds true of conversation, or especially written words, is true in prayer. We live in the generation when the Book of Common Prayer underwent the first substantial change since its publication in the seventeenth century. "Thee's" and "Thou's" have disappeared from most public prayers, replaced by "You's" and "Your's."

Dr. Watts reminds us not to rush into asking whatever we have on our heart, like children who cannot wait to greet their grandparents but immediately want to know where the next goody is to be found! Jesus taught us in His model prayer to begin with concern with God's concerns: "Hallowed be thy name. Thy kingdom come, thy will be done on earth as it is in heaven."

In taking seriously the instruction to purposely include such elements as adoration and confession, we gradually train ourselves not to use prayer as a way of simply getting what we want from the Lord. Praying has as much to do with changing our hearts and correcting our perspectives as it has to do with seeking and finding answers to our particular needs.

In praying with small groups, it is easy to copy styles of praying, however unsuitable they may actually be. "Lord, we just ask you . . ." is one phrase that is sometimes much overused. We do learn by hearing, and it is a recognition of the dignity and majesty of God to seek to let our language in public prayer uphold the vision of that majesty we find in the Scriptures and in the written prayers of our forebears in the faith.

In spite of the passage of years and generations, the heart and soul of Isaac Watts still speaks a clear and needed word to us as we seek to learn to pray.

—Hal M. Helms

About This Edition

The text of Watts's guide to prayer was established from a version published in 1832 by Lincoln and Edmands of Boston as one of three "Aids to Devotion." An abridged version published in the early twentieth century by The Epworth Press of London was used for comparison.

The commentary following each chapter underscores the relevance of the text to our twentieth and twenty-first century needs.

May the power of Dr. Watts's guide to prayer speak clearly to seekers in our time who yearn to commune with him whose love, so amazing, so divine, demands our soul, our life, our all.

Preface

The duty of prayer is so great and necessary a part of religion that every degree of assistance toward the discharge of it will be always acceptable to pious minds. The inward and spiritual performance of this worship is taught us in many excellent discourses; but a regular scheme of prayer, as a Christian exercise, or a piece of holy skill, has been much neglected. The form, method, and expression of prayer, together with other attendants of it, such as voice and gesture, have been so little treated of, that few Christians have any clear or distinct knowledge of them. And yet all these have too powerful an influence upon the soul in its most spiritual exercises, and they properly fall under various directions of nature and Scripture. Now, while *institutions* of Logic and Rhetoric abound, that teach us to reason aright, and to speak well among men, why should the *rules of speaking* to God be so much untaught?

It is a glory to our profession that there is a great number of ministers in our day and nation who are happy in the gift of prayer, and exercise it continually in an honorable and useful manner. Yet they have been contented to direct others to this attainment merely by the influence of a good example. Thus, we are taught to pray as some profess to teach French and Latin, i.e., only by *rote*; whereas those that learn by rule as well as by imitation acquire a great readiness of just and proper expression in speaking those languages upon every occasion.

I am persuaded that one reason of this neglect has been the angry zeal for parties among us, which has discouraged men of sober and moderate principles from attempting much on this subject, while the zealots have been betrayed into two extremes. Some contend earnestly for pre-composed set forms of prayer, and will worship no other way. These have little need of any other instructions but to be taught to read well, since the words, matter, and method of their prayers are already appointed. Other violent men, in extreme opposition to them, have indulged the irregular wanderings of thought and expression, lest by a confinement to rules, they should seem to restrain the Spirit, and return to carnal ordinances.

But, if the leaders of one party had spent as much time in learning to pray as they have done in reading liturgies and vindicating their imposition, and if the warm writers of the other side, together with their just cautions against quenching the Spirit, had more cultivated this divine skill themselves and taught Christians regularly how to pray, I believe the practice of *free prayer* would have been more universally approved, and the fire of this controversy would never have raged to the destruction of so much charity.

My design in this treatise has been to write a *Prayer book without forms.* I have sought to maintain the middle way between the distant mistakes of contending Christians.

In describing the *nature of the duty of prayer*, though I have not enlarged much on each particular nor multiplied subdivisions, yet I have endeavored with the utmost care and exactness to divide the duty into all its necessary parts, that the memory of young Christians might be always furnished with some proper matter and method for their addresses to God.

The Gift, Grace, and Spirit of Prayer have of late years been made the subject of plentiful ridicule. And while some have utterly abandoned all pretenses to them and turned the very terms to jest and reproach, it must be confessed that others have given too just occasion for such scandal by explaining all these words in so exalted a sense as befits nothing but Divine inspiration. I have endeavored, therefore, to reduce those terms to their more proper and rational meaning and to explain them in such a way as the wisest and best of men of all persuasions, who have not been warmed with party zeal, have generally allowed. And I have had this design in my view, that plainer Christians among the dissenters might understand what they themselves mean, when they speak of *praying by a gift*, and *praying by the Spirit*, so that they might not expose themselves to the censure of talking without meaning, nor be charged with enthusiasm by their conforming neighbors.

In discoursing of the *gift* or *ability* to pray, I have been large and particular both in directions to attain it and in describing the mistakes and indecencies that persons may be in danger of committing in this duty. I am well assured that we learn to avoid what is worthy of condemnation by a plain representation of the fault and follies, much better than by a bare proposal of the best rules and directions.

But here I am pressed between a double difficulty, and already I feel the pain of displeasing some of my readers.

If I should describe these improprieties of speech and action in a moderate degree, scoffers would reproach a whole party of Christians and say that I had copied all from the life; while my friends would be ready to suspect that I had published some of the errors of weaker brethren.

On the other hand, if I should represent these faults in their utmost degree of offensiveness, the adversary indeed could scarce have malice enough to believe any preacher in our day was guilty of them. But my friends would tell me I had played at impertinences by exposing such faults as nobody practices.

Now, when two evils lie before me, I would choose the least. It is better to be impertinent than a publisher of folly; and therefore I have set forth those indecencies in their very worst appearance, that they might never be practiced. Upon this account, I have been forced to borrow instances of improper expressions from antiquated writers and several of the descriptions of irregular voices and gestures from some obscure persons of the last age, whose talent of assurance was almost the only qualification that made them speakers in public. And this I was constrained to do because my observations of the prayers I have heard could never have supplied my design.

Besides, had I described some tolerable follies, perhaps weak men might have been ready to vindicate them because they did not see deformity enough to be blamed. But now the instances I have given appear so disagreeable and ridiculous that all men must be convinced they ought to be avoided; and younger Christians, when they learn to pray, will keep at the greatest distance from all such examples.

But 'tis a hard matter to attempt reformation of any kind without giving offense.

I have also added one short chapter on the Grace of prayer, that the work might not appear too imperfect, though that has been abundantly and happily pursued in many treatises and is the subject of daily sermons.

In speaking of the spirit of prayer, I have tried to obviate all controversies that have arisen to trouble the church by giving what appeared to me the most natural exposition of the chief Scriptures that refer to this matter, and adding a reasonable and intelligible account of what hand the Spirit of God may be supposed to have in assisting his people in this part of worship.

At the end of these chapters I have laid down many rules borrowed from reason, observation, and Holy Scripture, telling how every Christian may in some degree attain these desirable blessings. And I have concluded the whole with a hearty persuasive to covet the best gifts and seek after the most excellent way of the performance of this duty.

Perhaps some persons may wonder that in a treatise which professes to teach the skill of prayer, I should not once recommend the prayer that our Lord taught his disciples as a perfect pattern for all Christians. But it is my opinion that divine wisdom gave it for other purposes. And if this treatise meet with proper acceptance in the world, I may hereafter venture to expose my sentiments on the Lord's prayer, if God shall ever give me health to review and finish them, with a short essay or two on the personal ministry of Christ upon earth, which are proper to be joined with them.

These instructions were at first composed for the use of a private society of younger men who were desirous to learn to pray, and this may excuse the style and way of address in some parts of the discourse. It has lain silent by me several years and resisted many a call to appear in public, in hopes of being more polished before its first appearance. But when I shall have health and leisure to dress all my thoughts to the best advantage, that God only knows, whose hand has long confined me. I am convinced at last that it is better for me to do something for God, though it be attended with imperfections, than be guilty of perpetual delays in hopes of better pleasing myself.

After all the care I have taken to avoid controversy and to express myself in such a way as might not be justly offensive to any sober Christians, yet if I should prove so unhappy as to say any thing disagreeable to the sentiments of some of my younger readers, I must entreat them not to throw away the whole treatise and deprive themselves of all the benefit they might obtain by other parts of it. Nor should they load the whole book with reproaches and censures, lest thereby they prevent others from reaping those advantages towards converse with God which the more inoffensive pages might convey. An unwary censure or a rash and hasty word thrown upon a discourse, or a sermon, a preacher or a writer, hath sometimes done more disservice to religion than could ever be recompensed by many recantations. Permit, therefore, this little book, that has an honest design: to teach creatures to hold correspondence with their God. Permit it to do all the service it can.

Had I found any treatise that had answered my designs, I had never given myself the trouble of writing this at first nor ventured to expose it now. There are, indeed, several well composed forms of devotion in the world, written by ministers of the conformist and non-conformist persuasions. And these are of excellent use to instruct us in the matter and language of prayer, if we maintain our holy liberty and do not tie our thoughts down to the words of men. Mr. Henry's *Method of Prayer* is a judicious collection of Scriptures proper to the several parts of that duty. Mr. Murray has composed a volume of addresses to God, which he calls *Closet Devotions on the Principal Heads of Divinity, in the Expressions of Scripture.* Both these, if rightly used, will afford happy assistance to the humble and serious worshiper. Those *Six Sermons of Prayer,* published since this was written, are the useful labors of some of my valuable friends, and have many divine thoughts in them. But they take in the whole compass of this subject, in all the inward as well as outward part of the worship, and therefore could not allow sufficient room to enlarge upon that which is my great design.

It is not necessary therefore to inform the world that Bishop Wilkins, in his discourse of the *Gift of Prayer,* has been my chief assistant toward the second chapter of this book. Nor need I tell the reader what writings I have consulted of the learned and pious Dr. Owen and others that have written for or against the work of the Spirit in Prayer, in order to gain a clearer light. Nor need I tell what hints I have borrowed from the treatise of a very judicious author, with a fanciful title imposed upon it by an unknown hand, and called the *Generation of Seekers*. In it several practical cases about the *aids of the Spirit* are largely and well handled, though I had the opportunity of knowing and consulting it only since this was in the press.

But if there are any advances made here beyond the labors of great men in the last age, I hope the world will excuse this attempt. And if younger Christians, by perusal of these papers, shall find themselves improved in the holy skill of prayer when they get nearest the throne of grace, I entreat them to put in one petition for the author, who has languished under great weakness for some years past and is cut off from all public service. If ever he be restored again he shall rejoice in farther labors for their good; he shall share in the pleasure of their improvements and assist them in the work of praise.

—Isaac Watts

Introduction by Author

Prayer is a word of an extensive sense in Scripture, and includes not only a request or petition for mercies but is taken for the address of a creature on earth to God in heaven about everything that concerns his God, his neighbor or himself, in this world or the world to come. It is that concern which God hath allowed us to maintain with himself above while we are here below. It is that language wherein a creature holds correspondence with his Creator, and wherein the soul of a saint often gets near to God, is entertained with great delight, and, as it were, dwells with his heavenly Father for a short season before he comes to heaven. It is a glorious privilege that our Maker has indulged to us, and a necessary part of that obedience which he hath required of us at all times and seasons and in every circumstance of life—according to those Scriptures, I Thess. 5:17, "Pray without ceasing." Phil. 4:6, "In every thing by prayer and supplication, with thanksgiving, let your request be made known to God." Eph. 6:18, "Praying always, with prayer and supplication."

Prayer is a part of divine worship that is required of all men, and is to be performed either with the voice or only in the heart, and is called vocal or mental prayer. It is commanded to single persons in their private retirements, in a more solemn and continued method or manner—and, in the midst of the business of life, by secret and sudden liftings up of the soul to God. It belongs also to the communities of men, whether they be natural, as families, or civil, as corporations, parliaments, courts, or societies for trade and business, and to religious communities, as when persons meet on any pious design they should seek their God. It is required of the churches of

Christians in an especial manner, for the house of God is the house of prayer. Since, therefore, it is a duty of such absolute necessity for all men, and of such universal use, it is fit we should all know how to perform it aright, that it may obtain acceptance of the great God and become a delightful and profitable exercise to our own souls and to those that join with us.

To this end I shall deliver my thoughts on this subject in the following order:

First, I shall speak of the nature of prayer as a duty of worship.

Secondly, As it is to be performed by the gifts or abilities God has bestowed upon us.

Thirdly, As it must be attended with the exercise of our graces.

Fourthly, As we are assisted in it by the Spirit of God. And,

Fifthly, Conclude all with an earnest address to Christians to seek after this holy skill of converse with God.

—Isaac Watts

Contents

The Different Parts of Prayer

*I*n the discourse of prayer, considered as a duty of worship required of us, that we may understand the whole nature of it better, let it be divided into its several parts; and I think they may be all included in these following, namely:

Invocation, Adoration, Confession, Petition, Pleading, Profession or Self-dedication, Thanksgiving and Blessing:—of each of which I shall speak particularly.

Invocation

The first part of prayer is invocation, or calling upon God, and it may include in it these three things:

1. A making mention of one or more of the names or titles of God. And thus we do as it were address the person to whom we pray, as you have abundant instances in the prayers that are delivered to us in Holy Scripture; "O Lord my God, most high, and most holy God and Father." "O God of Israel, that dwellest between the cherubim." "Almighty God and everlasting King." "Our Father which art in heaven." "O God, that keepest covenant"; and several others.

2. A declaration of our desire and design to worship him. "Unto thee do we lift up our souls." "We draw near unto thee as our God." "We come into thy presence." "We that are but dust and ashes take upon us to speak to thy Majesty." "We bow ourselves before thee in humble addresses"; or suchlike. And here it may not be amiss to mention briefly one or two general expressions of our own unworthiness.

3. A desire of his assistance and acceptance, under a sense of our insufficiency and unworthiness, in such language as this is: "Lord, quicken us to call upon thy name." "Assist us by thy

Spirit in our access to thy mercy seat." "Raise our hearts towards thyself." "Teach us to approach thee as becomes creatures, and do thou draw near to us as a God of grace." "Hearken to the voice of my cry, my King and my God, for unto thee will I pray" (Psalm 5:2), in which words you have all these three parts of invocation expressed.

Adoration

The second part of prayer is adoration, or honor paid to God by the creature, and it contains these four things:

1. A mention of his nature as God, with the highest admiration and reverence. And this includes his most original properties and perfections, namely his self-sufficient existence, that he is God of and from himself, his unity of essence, that there is no other God besides himself, his inconceivable subsistence in three persons—the Father, the Son, and the Holy Spirit—which mystery of the Trinity is a most proper object of our adoration and wonder since it so much surpasses our understanding. His incomprehensible distance from all creatures, and his infinite superiority of nature above them, seems also to claim a place here. The language of this part of prayer runs thus: "Thou art God, and there is none else; thy name alone is Jehovah the Most High. Who in the heavens can be compared to the Lord, or who among the sons of the mighty can be likened to our God? All nations before thee are as nothing, and they are counted in thy sight less than nothing and vanity. Thou art the first and the last, the only true and living God; thy glorious name is exalted above all blessing and praise."

2. The mention of his several attributes with due expressions of praise, and with the exercise of suitable grace and affections, such as his power, his justice, his wisdom, his sov-

ereignty, his holiness, his goodness and mercy. Abundance of which sort of expressions you find in Scripture in those addresses that the saints have made to God in all ages. "Thou art very great, O Lord, thou art clothed with honor and majesty. Thou art the blessed and only King of kings, and Lord of lords. All things are naked and open before thine eyes. Thou searchest the heart of man, but how unsearchable is thine understanding? and thy power is unknown. Thou art of purer eyes than to behold iniquity. Thy mercy endureth forever. Thou art slow to anger, abundant in goodness, and thy truth reaches to all generations."

These meditations are of great use in the beginning of our prayers, to abase us before the throne of God, to awaken our reverence, our dependence, our faith and hope, our humility and our joy.

3. The mention of his several works, of creation, of providence, and of grace, with proper praises. For as God is glorious in himself, in his nature and attributes, so by the works of his hands hath he manifested that glory to us, and it becomes us to ascribe the same glory to him—that is, to tell him humbly what a sense we have of the several perfections he hath revealed in these works of his, in such language as this: "Thou, Lord, hast made the heavens and the earth. The whole creation is the work of thine hands. Thou rulest among the armies of heaven, and among the inhabitants of the earth thou doest what pleases thee. Thou hast revealed thy goodness towards mankind, and hast magnified thy mercy above all thy name. Thy works of nature and of grace are full of wonder, and sought out by all those that have pleasure in them."

4. The mention of his relation to us as Creator, as a Father, as a Redeemer, as a King, as an almighty Friend, and our everlasting inheritance. And here it will not be improper to make mention of the name of Christ, in and through whom alone we

are brought nigh to God, and made his children. By his incarnation and atonement he becomes a God and Father to sinful men and appears their reconciled Friend. And by this means we draw still nearer to God in every part of this work of adoration. When we consider his nature, we stand afar off from him as creatures from a God, for he is infinitely superior to us. When we speak of his attributes, there seems to grow a greater acquaintance between God and us, while we tell him we have learned something of his power, his wisdom, his justice, and his mercy. But when we proceed to make mention of the several works of his hand, wherein he hath sensibly discovered himself to our understandings, we seem yet to approach nigher to God, and when at last we can arise to call him our God, from a sense of his special relation to us in Christ, then we gain the nearest access; and are better prepared for the following parts of this worship.

Confession

The third part of prayer consists in confession, which may also be divided into these four headings:

1. A humble confession of the crudeness of our nature in its original; our distance from God, as we are creatures; our subjection to him, and our constant dependence on him. "Thou, O Lord, art in heaven, but we on the earth; our being is but of yesterday, and our foundation is in the dust. What is man that thou art mindful of him, and the son of man that thou shouldest visit him? Man that is a worm, and the son of man that is but a worm! It is in thee that we live, move and have our being—if thou withholdest thy breath, we die."

2. A confession of our sins—both original, which belong to our nature, and actual, that have been found in the course

of our lives. We should confess our sins under the sense of the guilt of them, as well as under the deep and mournful impressions of the power of sin in our hearts. We should confess the sins that we have been guilty of in thought, as well as the iniquities of our lips and of our lives. We should confess our sins of omission and sins of commission, the sins of our childhood and of our riper years, sins against the law of God, and sins more particularly committed against the gospel of our Lord Jesus Christ.

Sometimes it is convenient and necessary to enter into a more particular detail of our various faults and follies. We should mourn before God because of our pride and vanity of mind, the violence of our passions, our earthly-mindedness and love of this world, our sensuality and indulgence of our flesh, our carnal security and unthankfulness under plentiful mercies, our sinful dejection in a time of trouble, our neglect of duty and want of love to God, our unbelief and hardness of heart, our slothfulness and decay in religion, the dishonors we have brought to God, and all our miscarriages towards our fellow creatures. And these may be aggravated on purpose to humble our souls yet more before God, by a reflection on their variety and their multitude. How often they have been repeated even before and since we knew God savingly. We have committed them against much light, and we have sinned against much love—and that after many rebukes of the word and providence, and many consolations from the gospel and Spirit of God. You find this part of prayer very plentifully insisted and enlarged upon among those examples that are left us in the word of God. And with these confessions we must thus bewail and take shame to ourselves. "We are ashamed and blush to lift up our faces before thee, our God, for our iniquities are increased over our head and our trespasses grown up to the heavens. Behold we are vile, what shall we answer thee?

We will lay our hands upon our mouth, and put our mouth in the dust if so be there may be hope."

3. A confession of our deserving of punishment and our unworthiness of mercy, arising from the sense that we have of all our aggravated sins, in such expressions as these: "We deserve, O Lord, to be forever cast out of thy presence, and to be eternally cut off from all hope of mercy. We deserve to fall under the curse of that law which we have broken and to be forever banished from the blessings of that gospel which we have so long refused. We have sinned against so much mercy that we are no longer worthy to be called thy children. We are utterly unworthy of any of those favors that are promised in thy word and which thou hast given us encouragement to hope for. If thou contend with us for our transgressions, we are not able to answer thee, O Lord, nor to make excuse for one of a thousand. If thou shouldest mark iniquities, O Lord, who shall stand? But there is forgiveness with thee, there is mercy and plenteous redemption."

4. A confession or humble representation of our wants and sorrows of every kind, the particulars of which will fall under the next heading. But it is necessary that they should be spread before God and poured out as it were in his presence, for God loves to hear us tell him what a sense our souls have of our own particular necessities and troubles. He loves to hear us complain before him when we are under any pressures from his hand, or when we stand in need of mercies of any kind.

Petition

The fourth part of prayer consists in petition, which includes in it a desire of deliverance from evil and a request of good things to be bestowed. And on both these accounts we must offer up our petitions to God for ourselves and our fellow creatures.

The evils we pray to be delivered from are of a temporal, spiritual, or eternal kind. "O Lord, take away the guilt of our sins by the atonement of thine own Son. Subdue the power of our iniquities by thine own Spirit. Deliver us from the natural darkness of our own minds, from the corruption of our hearts, and from the perverse tendencies of our appetites and passions. Free us from the temptations to which we are exposed and the daily snares that attend us. We are in constant danger whilst we are in this life; let the watchful eye of our God be upon us for our defense. Deliver us from thine everlasting wrath. Save us from the power of our enemies in this world, and from all the painful evils that we have justly exposed ourselves to by sinning against thee."

The good we desire to be conferred upon us is also of a temporal, spiritual, or eternal nature. As we pray for the pardon of all our iniquities for the sake of the great atonement— the death of our Redeemer—so we beg of God the justification of our persons through the righteousness of his own Son Jesus Christ, and our acceptance with God unto eternal life. We pray for the sanctification of our natures by his Holy Spirit and for his enlightening influences to teach us the knowledge of God in Christ Jesus, as well as to reveal to us the evil of sin and our danger by it. We pray for the consolation of the Spirit of God, and that he would not only work faith and love and every grace in our hearts, but give us bright and plentiful evidences of his own work, and of our own interest in the love of God. We say unto God: "O thou that hast the hearts of all men in thine hand, form our hearts according to thine own will, and according to the image of thine own Son. Be thou our light and our strength, make us run in the ways of holiness. And let all the means of grace be continued to us, and be made serviceable for the great end for which thou hast appointed them. Preserve thy gospel amongst us, and let all thy providence be sanctified.

"Let thy mercies draw us nearer to thyself, as with the cords of love; and let the several strokes of thine afflicting hand wean us from sin, mortify us to this world, and make us ready for a departure hence whensoever thou pleasest to call us. Guide us by thy counsels and secure us by thy grace in all our travels through this dangerous wilderness, and at last give us a triumph over death and a rich and abundant entrance into the kingdom of thy Son in glory. But since while we are here we wear these bodies of flesh about us, and there are many things necessary to support our lives and to make them easy and comfortable, we entreat thou wouldst bestow these conveniences and refreshments upon us so far as is consistent with thine own glory and the designs of thy grace. Let our health, our strength, and our peace be maintained, and let holiness to the Lord be inscribed upon them all, that whatsoever we receive from thy hands may be improved to thine honor and our own truest advantage; heal our diseases and pardon our iniquities, that our souls may ever bless thee."

And as we are required to offer up petitions for ourselves and make our own requests known to God, so we are commanded to make supplication for all saints (Ephesians 6:18) and to offer up prayers and intercessions for all men (1 Timothy 2:1). And the word "intercession" is the common name for this part of our petitions. In general, we must pray for the church of Christ, for Zion lies near to the heart of God, and her name is written upon the palms of the hands of our Redeemer. The welfare of Zion should be much upon our hearts; we ought ever to have the tenderest concern for the whole church of God in the world. His church he values above kingdoms and nations, and therefore if we distinguish degrees of fervency in prayer, we ought to plead more earnestly with God for his church than for any nation or kingdom—that he would enlarge the borders of the dominion of Christ, that he would spread his gospel among the heathens and make the name of Christ known and glorious from the rising of the sun to its going down, that he would call in the remainder of his ancient people the Jews, and bring the fullness of the Gentiles into his church, that he would pour down a more abundant measure of his own Spirit to carry on his work upon the earth. And we are to send up longing and earnest wishes to heaven that the Spirit may descend and be diffused in plentiful degree upon churches, upon ministers, upon families, and upon all the saints. We are to pray that God would deliver his church from the power of persecuting enemies, that he would restrain the wrath of man, and suffer not the wicked to triumph over the righteous. We are also in particular to request of God mercy for the nation to which we belong, that liberty and peace may be established and flourish in it, and for governors that rule over us in places of supreme authority or subordinate—that wisdom and faithfulness may be conferred upon them from heaven to manage those affairs God hath entrusted them with on earth. We must pray for our friends and those that are nearly related to us, that God would deliver them from all the evils they feel or fear and bestow upon them all the good we wish for ourselves here or hereafter.

There is also another kind of petition which is used frequently in the Old Testament, and that is calling for vengeance and destruction upon enemies. But this is very seldom to be used under the gospel, which is a dispensation of love, and should never be employed against our personal enemies but only against the enemies of Christ and such as are irreconcilable to him. Christ has taught us in his life and given us an example at his death to forgive and pray for our personal enemies, for that is a noble singularity and glory of our religion.

Here let it be observed that when we pray for those things which are absolutely necessary to the glory of God or to our own salvation, we may use a more full and fervent importunity in prayer. We may say, "Lord, without the pardon of our sins we cannot rest satisfied. Without the renovation of our natures by thy grace, our souls can never rest easy. Without the hopes of heaven we can never be at peace, and in these respects will never let thee go till thou bless us. For Zion's sake we will not hold our peace, and for the sake of thy Jerusalem, thy glory, thy church in the world, we will give thee no rest till thou hast made her the joy of the earth." But on the other hand, when we plead with God for those mercies or comforts upon which our salvation or his own glory do not necessarily depend, we dare not use so absolute an importunity in prayer; but we must learn to limit our petitions in such language as this: "If it be consistent with thine eternal counsels, with the purposes of grace and the great ends of thy glory, then bestow upon us such a blessing. If it may be for the true interest of our souls and for thine honor in the world, then let this favor be granted to us. Otherwise we would learn to resign ourselves to thy wiser determination and say, 'Father, not our wills, but thine be done.'"

Pleading

The fifth part of prayer may be called pleading with God. Though it be not so distinct a part by itself, but rather belongs to the work of petition and request, yet it is so very large and diffusive, that it may well be separated by itself, and treated of distinctly. Pleading with God or arguing our case with him in a fervent, yet humble manner, is one part of that importunity in prayer which Scripture so much recommends. This is what all the saints of old have practiced, and what Job resolves to engage in (Job 23:4): "If I could get nearer to God, I would order my cause before him, and fill my mouth with arguments." This is what the prophet Jeremiah practices (Jeremiah 12:1): "Righteous art thou, O Lord, when I plead with thee, yet let me talk with thee of thy judgments; wherefore doth the way of the wicked prosper?" We are not to suppose that our arguments can have any real influence on God's own will, and persuade him contrary to what he was before inclined. But as he condescends to talk with us after the manner of men, so he admits us to talk with him in the same manner too, and encourages us to plead with him as though he were inwardly and really moved and prevailed upon by our importunities. So you find Moses is said to have prevailed upon God for the preservation of his people Israel, when he seemed resolved upon their destruction (Exodus 32:7-14).

In this work of pleading with God, arguments are almost infinite, but the chief of them may be reduced to these following headings:

1. We may plead with God from the greatness of our needs, our dangers, or our sorrows; whether they relate to the soul or the body, to this life or the life to come, to ourselves or those for whom we pray. We may draw arguments for deliverance from the particular kind of afflictions that we labor under. "My sorrows, O Lord, are such as overpress me and endanger my dishonoring of thy name and thy gospel. My pains and my weaknesses hinder me from thy service, so that I am rendered useless upon earth and a cumberer of the ground. They have been already of so long continuance that I fear my flesh will not be able to hold out, nor my spirit to bear up, if thine hand abide thus heavy upon me. If this sin be not subdued in me or that temptation removed, I fear that I shall

be turned aside from the paths of religion and let go my hope." Thus from the kind, degree, or duration of our difficulties, we may draw arguments for relief.

2. The several perfections of the nature of God are another heading of arguments in prayer. "For thy mercies' sake, O Lord, save me; thy loving kindness is infinite, let this infinite loving kindness be displayed in my salvation. Thou art wise, O Lord, and though mine enemies are crafty, thou canst disappoint their devices, and thou knowest how by thy wondrous counsels to turn my sorrows into joy. Thou canst find out a way for my relief, when all creatures stand afar off and say that they see no way to help me. Thou art almighty and all-sufficient. Thy power can suppress my adversaries at once, vanquish the tempter, break the powers of darkness to pieces, release me from the chains of corruption, and bring me into glorious liberty. Thou art just and righteous—and wilt thou let the enemy oppress forever? Thou art sovereign, and all things are at thy command. Thou canst say to pains and diseases, 'go,' or 'come'; speak therefore the sovereign word of healing and my flesh and soul shall praise thee. Thou delightest in pardoning grace. It is the honor of our God to forgive; therefore let my iniquities be all canceled, through the abundance of thy rich mercy."

3. Another argument in pleading with God may be drawn from the several relations in which God stands unto men, particularly to his own people. "Lord, thou art my Creator, wilt thou not have a desire to the work of thine hands? Hast thou not made me and fashioned me, and wilt thou destroy me? Thou art my Governor and my King; to whom should I fly for protection but to thee, when the enemies of thine honor and my soul beset me around? Art thou not my Father?—and hast thou not called me one of thy children and given me a name and a place among thy sons and thy daughters? Why should I

look like one cast out of thy sight, or one that belongs to the family of Satan? Dost thou not have the tender feelings and compassions of a father? Why should one of thy poor, weak, helpless children be neglected or forgotten? Art thou not my God in covenant, and the God and Father of my Lord Jesus Christ, by whom that covenant is ratified? Under that relation I would plead with thee for all necessary mercies."

4. The various and particular promises of the covenant of grace are another rank of arguments to use in prayer. "Enlighten me, O Lord, and pardon me, and sanctify my soul; and bestow grace and glory upon me according to that word of thy promise on which thou hast caused me to hope. Remember thy word is past in heaven. It is recorded among the articles of thy sweet covenant that I must receive light and love, and strength and joy, and happiness. And art thou not a faithful God to fulfil every one of those promises? What if heaven and earth must pass away? Yet thy covenant stands upon two immutable pillars: thy promise and thine oath. And now I have fled for refuge to lay hold on this hope. Let me have strong consolation. Remember the covenant made with thy Son in the days of eternity, and let the mercies there promised to all his seed be bestowed upon me according to my various needs." Calling to remembrance the covenant of God hath been often of great efficacy and prevalence in the prayers of the ancient saints.

5. The name and honor of God in the world is another powerful argument. "What wilt thou do for thy great name, if Israel be cut off or perish?" (Joshua 7:9). "If thy saints go down to the grave in multitudes, who shall praise thee in the land of the living? The dead cannot celebrate thee, nor make mention of thy name and honors, as I do this day." This was the pleading of Hezekiah (Isaiah 38:18). And David uses the same language (Psalm 6:5). "For thy name's sake," was

almighty argument in all the ancient times of the church.

6. Former experiences of ourselves and others are another set of arguments to make use of in prayer. Our Lord Jesus Christ in that prophetical psalm, Psalm 22:5, is represented as using this argument: "Our fathers cried unto thee, O Lord, and were delivered; they trusted in thee, and they were not confounded. Let me be a partaker of the same favor whilst I cry unto thee, and make thee my trust. Thou hast never said to the seed of Jacob, 'Seek ye my face in vain'; and let it not be said that thy poor servant has now sought thy face and has not found thee. Often have I received mercy in a way of return to prayer; often hath my soul drawn near unto thee, and been comforted in the midst of sorrows. Often have I taken out fresh supplies of grace according to my need from the treasures of thy grace that are in Christ—and shall the door of those treasures be shut against me now? Shall I receive no more favors from the hand of my God, that has heretofore dealt them so plentifully to me?"

Now how improper soever this sort of argument may seem to be used in courts of princes or to entreat the favor of great men, yet God loves to hear his own people make use of it. For though men are quickly weary of multiplying their bounties, yet the more we receive from God, if we humbly acknowledge it to him, the more we are like to receive still.

7. The most powerful and most prevailing argument is the name and mediation of our Lord Jesus Christ. And though there be some hints or shadows of it in the Old Testament, yet it was never taught us in a plain and express manner till a little before our Saviour left this world (John 16:23, 24), "Hitherto ye have asked nothing in my name. Ask and ye shall receive, that your joy may be full. Whatsoever ye shall ask the Father in my name, he will give it you." This seems to be reserved for the peculiar pleasure and power of the duty of prayer under the

gospel. We are taught to make mention of the name of Jesus, the only begotten and eternal Son of God, as a method to receive our biggest requests and fullest salvation. And in such language as this we should address the Father: "Lord, let my sins be forgiven for the sake of that love which thou bearest to thine own Son; for the sake of that love which thy Son beareth to thee for the sake of his humble state, when he took flesh upon him that he might look like a sinner, and be made a sacrifice, though himself was free from sin; for the sake of his perfect and painful obedience, which has given complete honor to thy law; for the sake of the curse which he bore, and the death which he suffered, and honored thy justice more than it was possible for my sins to have affronted it. Remember his dying groans, remember his agonies when the hour of darkness was upon him, and let not the powers of darkness prevail over me. Remember the day when thou stoodest afar from thine own Son, and he cried out as one forsaken of God, and let me have thine everlasting presence with me. Let me never be forsaken, since thy Son hath borne that punishment."

Again we may plead with God the intercession of Jesus our High Priest above: "Father, we would willingly ask thee for nothing but what thy Son already asks thee for. We would willingly request nothing at thine hands but what thine own Son requests beforehand for us. Look upon the Lamb, as he had been slain, in the midst of the throne. Look upon his pure and perfect righteousness and on that blood with which our High Priest is entered into the highest heavens, and in which forever he appears before thee to make intercession. And let every blessing be bestowed upon us, which that blood did purchase, and which that great, that infinite Petitioner pleads for at thy right hand. What canst thou deny thine own Son? for he hath told us, that thou hearest him always. For the sake of that Son of thy love, deny us not."

Thus I have finished this fifth part of prayer, which consists in pleading with God.

Profession, or Self-dedication

The sixth part of prayer consists in a profession or self dedication. This is very seldom mentioned by writers as a part of prayer; but to me it appears so very necessary in its nature, and so distinct from all the rest, that it ought to be treated of separately as well as any other part; and may be divided under these four headings:

1. A profession of our relation to God. And it is worthwhile sometimes for a saint to draw near unto God, and to tell him that he is the Lord's; that he belongs to his family; that he is one of his household; that he stands among the number of his children; that his name is written in his covenant. A great deal of spiritual delight and soul-satisfaction arises from such appeals to God concerning our relation to him.

2. A profession of our former transactions with God. "Lord, we have given ourselves up to thee, and chosen thee for our eternal inheritance and our highest good; we have seen the insufficiency of creatures to make us happy, and we have betaken ourselves to a higher hope; we have beheld Christ Jesus the Savior in his perfect righteousness, and in his all-sufficient grace; we have put our trust in him, and we have made our covenant with the Father, by the sacrifice of the Son; we have often drawn near to thee in thine ordinances; we have ratified and confirmed the holy covenant at thy table, as well as been devoted to thee by the initial ordinance of baptism; we have given up our names to God in his house; and we have, as it were, subscribed with our hands to be the Lord's."

3. A present surrender of ourselves to God, and a profes-

sion of our several affections and graces toward him. And this is sweet language in prayer, when the soul is in a right frame. "Lord, I confirm all my former dedications of myself to thee; and let all my covenantings be forever ratified, or if I did never yet sincerely give myself up to the Lord, I do it now with the greatest solemnity, and from the bottom of my heart. I commit my guilty soul into the hands of Jesus my Redeemer, that he may sprinkle it with his atoning blood, that he may clothe it with his justifying righteousness, and make me, a vile sinner, accepted in the presence of a just and holy God. I appear, O Father, in the presence of thy justice and holiness, clothed in the garments of thine own Son. I give my soul, that has much corruption in it by nature, and much of the remaining power of sin, into the hands of my almighty Savior, that by his grace he may form all my powers anew; that he may subdue every irregular appetite, and root out every disorderly passion; that he may frame me after his own image, fill me with his own grace, and fit me for his own glory. I hope in thee, my God, for thou art my refuge, my strength, and my salvation. I love thee above all things; and I know I love thee. Whom have I in heaven but thee? And there is none upon earth that I desire in comparison of thee. I desire thee with my strongest affections, and I delight in thee above all delights. My soul stands in awe, and fears before thee. And I rejoice to love such a God who is almighty, and the object of my highest reverence."

4. A profession of our humble and holy resolutions to be the Lord's forever. This is what is generally called a vow. Now, though I cannot encourage Christians to bind themselves in particular instances by frequently repeated vows, and especially in things that are in themselves indifferent, which oftentimes prove a dangerous snare to souls, yet we can never be too frequent or too solemn in the general surrender of our souls to God and binding our souls by a vow to be the Lord's forever—

to love him above all things, to fear him, to hope in him, to walk in his ways, in a course of holy obedience, and to wait for his mercy unto eternal life.

For such a vow as this is, is included in the nature of both the ordinances of the gospel, baptism, and the Lord's Supper. Such a vow as this is, is comprehended almost in every act of worship, and especially in solemn addresses to God by prayer. I might add, in the last place, that together with this profession or self-dedication to God, it is necessary we should renounce everything that is inconsistent herewith, and that under each of these four preceding headings: "As I am Thine, O Lord, and I belong not to this world, I have given myself to thee, and I have given myself away from sin and from the creature. I have renounced the world as my inheritance, and chosen the Father. I have renounced all other saviors, and all my own duties and righteousnesses as the foundation of my interest in the favor of God, and have chosen Christ Jesus as my only way to the Father. I have renounced my own strength as the ground of my hope—for my understanding is dark, my will is impotent, and my best affections are insufficient to carry me onwards to heaven. I now again renounce dependence upon all of them, that I may receive greater light and strength and love from God. I am dead to the law, I am mortified to sin, I am crucified to the world, and all by the Cross of Jesus my Savior. I bid Satan get him behind me; I renounce him and his works. I will neither fear him nor love him, nor lay a confederacy with the men of this world, for I love my God, for I fear my God, in my God is my eternal help and hope. I will say, "what have I to do any more with idols?" and I will banish the objects of temptation from my sight. Thus I abandon everything that would divide me from God, to whom I have made a surrender of myself. Shouldest thou deny me the particular requests I have presented to thee, I leave myself in thy hands, trusting thou wilt choose better for me. And because I know my own frailty of heart and the inconstancy of my will, I humbly put all these my vows and solemn arguments into the hands of my Lord Jesus to fulfil them in me and by me, through all the days of my infirmity and this dangerous state of trial."

Thanksgiving

The seventh part of prayer consists in thanksgiving. To give thanks is to acknowledge the bounty of that hand whence we receive our blessing, and to ascribe honor and praise to the power, the wisdom, and the goodness of God upon that account. And this is part of that tribute which God our King expects at our hands for all the favors we receive from him. It very ill becomes a creature to partake of benefits from his God, and then to forget his heavenly Benefactor, and grow regardless of that bounty whence his comforts flow. The matter of our thanksgivings may be ranged under these two headings: we must give thanks for those benefits for which we have prayed, and for those which God hath conferred upon us without our praying for them.

1. Those benefits which God hath bestowed on us without asking are proper to be mentioned in the first place, for they are the effects of his rich and prevenient mercy: and how many are the blessings of his goodness with which he hath preceded us! "We praise thee, O Lord, for thine original designs of love to fallen man, and that thou shouldest make a distinction between us and the angels that sinned. What is man, that thou art thoughtful about his salvation, and sufferest the angels to perish forever without remedy? that thou shouldest choose a certain number of the race of Adam, and give them into the hands of Christ Jesus, that their happiness might be secured, that thou shouldest reveal this mercy in various types and

promises to our fathers by the prophets, and that in thine own appointed time thou shouldest send thy Son to take our nature upon him, and to redeem us by his death? We give glory to thy justice and to thy grace for this work of terror and compassion, this work of reconciling sinners to thyself. . . .

"We praise thee for the gospel which thou hast published to the world, the gospel of pardon and peace; and that thou hast confirmed it by such abundant testimonies, to raise and establish our faith. We give glory to that power of thine that has guarded thy gospel in all ages, and through ten thousand oppositions of Satan has delivered it down safe to our age, and has proclaimed the glad tidings of peace in our nation. We bless thee that thou hast built habitations for thyself amongst us, and that we should be born in such a land of light as this is. It is a distinguishing favor of thine that among the works of thy creation we should be placed in the rank of rational beings. But it is more distinguishing goodness that we should be born of religious parents under the general promises of grace. We give thanks unto thy goodness for our preservation from many dangers which we could never foresee, and which we could not ask thee to prevent. How infinitely are we indebted to thee, O Lord, that our education should be under religious care and that we should have so many conveniences and comforts of life conferred upon us, as well as the means of grace brought near to us; and all this before we began to know thee or sought any of the mercies of this life or the other at thine hands."

2. We must give thanks for the benefits we have received as an answer to prayer. Whatsoever blessings we have sought at the hands of God demand our acknowledgments to his goodness when we become receivers. And here there is no need to enlarge in particulars, for we may look back upon the fourth part of prayer, which consists in petition, and there read

the matter of our thankfulness. There we learn to give glory to God for our deliverance from evils temporal and spiritual, and our hopes of deliverance from the evils that are eternal; for the communication of good for soul and body, and our comfortable expectation of the eternal happiness of both; for mercies bestowed on churches, on nations, on our governors, on relatives and our friends, as well as ourselves. And we should rejoice in our praises, and say to the Lord, "Verily thou art a God that hearest prayer, and thou hast not despised the cry of those that sought thee; we ourselves are witnesses that thou dost not bid thy people seek thy face in vain."

All these our thanksgivings may be yet farther heightened in prayer by the consideration of the multitude of the mercies that we have received, of their greatness, and of their continuance, by the mention of the glory and self-sufficiency of God the giver: that he is happy in himself, and stands in no need of us, and yet he condescends to confer perpetual benefits upon us; that he is sovereign, and might dispose of his favors to thousands, and leave us out of the number of his favorites; that we are as vile and unworthy as others, and that our God beholds all our unworthiness, all our guilt, our repeated provocations, and his past mercies abused, and yet he continues to have mercy upon us, and waits to be gracious.

Blessing

The eighth part of prayer consists in blessing of God, which has a distinct sense from praise or adoration, and is distinguished also from thanksgiving. In Psalm 145:10, it is said, "All thy works praise thee, and thy saints bless thee"—that is, even the inanimate creation, which are the works of God, manifest his attributes and his praises, but his saints do something more: they bless his name; which part of worship consists in these two things:

1. In mentioning the several attributes and glories of God with inward joy, satisfaction, and pleasure. "We delight, O Lord, to see thy name honored in the world, and we rejoice in thy real excellencies. We take pleasure to see thee exalted above all, we triumph in the several perfections of thy nature, and we give thanks at the remembrance of thine holiness." Thus we rejoice and bless the Lord for what he is in himself, as well as for what he has done for us, and this is a most divine and unselfish act of worship.

2. Wishing the glories of God may forever continue, and rejoicing at the assurance of it. "May the name of God be forever blessed. May the kingdom, and the power, and the glory be forever ascribed to him. May all generations call him honorable, and make his name glorious in the earth. To thee, O Father, Son, and Holy Spirit, belong everlasting power and honor."

Amen, or the Conclusion

We are taught in several places of Scripture to conclude our prayers with Amen, which is a Hebrew word that signifies truth, or faithfulness, certainly, surely, etc., and it implies in it these four things:

1. A belief of all that we have said concerning God and ourselves, of all our ascriptions of honor to God in the mention of his name, and attributes, and works, and a sensible inward persuasion of our own unworthiness, our wants and our sorrows which we have before expressed.

2. A wishing and desiring to obtain all that we have prayed for, longing after it, and looking for it. "Lord, let it be thus as

we have said" is the language of this little word "Amen" in the end of our prayers.

3. A confirmation of all our professions, promises, and engagements to God. It is used as the form of the oath of God in some places in Scripture. And it is as it were a solemn oath in our lips, binding ourselves to the Lord, according to the professions that we have made in the foregoing part of worship.

4. It implies also the hope and sure expectation of the acceptance of our persons, and the hearing of our prayers. For while we thus confirm our dedication of ourselves to God, we also humbly lay claim to his accomplishment of the promises of his covenant, and expect and wait that he will fulfil all our petitions, so far as they are agreeable to our truest interest and the designs of his own glory.

Prayer: Adoration and Praise

*"[In the Holy Scriptures, prayer] includes not
only a request or petition for mercies but is
taken for the address of a creature on earth to
God in heaven about everything that concerns
his God, his neighbor or himself, in this world
or the world to come. It is that concern which
God hath allowed us to maintain with himself
above, while we are here below. It is that
language wherein a creature holds correspondence with his Creator."* (Page xvii)

It is apparent that Isaac Watts was concerned with the
quality of worship and prayer in the churches of his time. As
a member of an Independent church, the worship he experienced was roughly equivalent to that of Puritan worship in
early America. There would be no musical instruments of any
kind, no prayer book out of which were read set prayers, and
no strict liturgy to be followed. Prayer would be led by the
minister, praying extemporaneously, or by one of the laymen.
Preaching would be the main focus of the service, and the sermons tended to be lengthy and full of carefully thought-out
doctrine.

In addition to the public worship, there were other occasions of prayer with which Dr. Watts was concerned. There
were informal meetings when friends and colleagues prayed
together. There were the daily prayers of "households"
which included the children and the servants in those homes
able to afford such. Again, our author was concerned that
such prayers be more than "off-the-cuff," awkward, and self-
conscious attempts. He strongly felt that such a high privilege
and awesome duty required the best.

Are such concerns relevant to us today? Does it matter what we say in prayer before God and before others? I think it does, and a lifetime of experience confirms that we often fall short in making our prayers reflect the seriousness and the dignity that should mark them.

We no longer kneel before kings and emperors. We make ourselves comfortable in the house of God. Air conditioning, pew cushions, soft lights, and soothing music are not uncommon. Gone are the crude, unpainted meetinghouses where our forebears worshiped. The awe-inspiring and dizzying apses of basilicas and cathedrals now are more for the eyes of tourists than for worshipers. Their high altars are frequently replaced by one nearer the people and on their level. Informality reigns where once majestic images reminded us that adoration and praise befit the creature as we come to worship the Creator.

Adoration [is the] honor paid to God by the creature.

Can there be any real worship or any real prayer without the heart's adoration of our loving Creator? Can we dare say that we have come into his presence without knowing that we have approached a mystery, a majesty, and a Being who is infinitely greater than ourselves? When Moses turned aside to see the bush that burned but was not consumed, he was told, "Take your shoes off your feet, for the place where you stand is holy ground."

> The Lord Jehovah reigns,
>   His throne is built on high;
> The garments he assumes
>   Are light and majesty;
> His glories shine with beams so bright,
> No mortal eye can bear the sight.

The thunders of his hand
  Keep the wide world in awe;
His wrath and justice stand
  To guard his holy law;
And where his love resolves to bless,
His truth confirms and seals the grace.

Through all his mighty works
  Amazing wisdom shines;
Confounds the powers of hell,
  And breaks their dark designs;
Strong is his arm, and shall fulfill
His great decrees and sovereign will.

And will this sovereign King
  Of glory condescend?
And will he write his name,
  My Father and my Friend?
I love his name, I love his word;
Join all my powers to praise the Lord!

Watts's hymns and psalms put a new song into the mouths of God's people. What he says here about the importance of adoration is amplified in many of his songs. In this way he helped people to experience the gift of praise as individuals and as congregations.

We greatly need to have our hearts expanded when we approach the place of prayer. Our tightly knit bundles often extend no farther than that of the man who prayed for "me, my wife, my son John, his wife, us four, no more." Praise is a way of expanding the heart, of aligning our concerns with God's concerns. That is why in his great model prayer, our Lord taught us to begin by saying, "Our Father who art in heaven, hallowed be thy name." All at once our concerns take a back seat. God's name, God's glory, God's will and God's purposes, take the foreground. We are in the business of aligning our thought with his.

Praise, prosaic as it may be, is a way of enlarging our interests and aligning them with God. By making our petitions and intercessions wait, we are putting things in better order. We cannot act like children who burst into the room with their wants without saying "Good morning." Praise is a corrective to our egocentric attitudes.

> Praise ye the Lord! 'tis good to raise
>   Your hearts and voices in his praise.
> His nature and his works invite
>   To make this duty our delight.
>
> He formed the stars, those heavenly flames,
>   He counts their numbers, calls their names;
> His wisdom's vast, and knows no bound,
>   A deep where all our thoughts are drowned.
>
> Sing to the Lord; exalt him high,
>   Who spreads his clouds along the sky,
> There he prepares the fruitful rain,
>   Nor lets the drops descend in vain.
>
> He makes the grass the hills adorn,
>   And clothes the smiling fields with corn;
> The beasts with food his hands supply,
>   And the young ravens when they cry.
>
> But saints are lovely in his sight,
>   He views his children with delight;
> He sees their hope, he knows their fear,
>   And looks and loves his image there.

Our churches still sing the words of hymns like these:

> From all that dwell below the skies,
>> Let the Creator's praise arise;
> Let the Redeemer's name be sung,
>> Through every land, by every tongue.
>
> Eternal are thy mercies, Lord;
>> Eternal truth attends thy word:
> Thy praise shall sound from shore to shore,
>> Till suns shall rise and set no more.

In another hymn Watts says,

> Wide as the world is thy command;
>> Vast as eternity thy love;
> Firm as a rock thy truth shall stand,
>> When rolling years have ceased to move.

Notice how the words carry one's mind away from the petty and parochial concerns of the moment, and lift the spirit into the vastness of God's eternity and his purposes. Surely we can agree with our author when he says, *Adoration is the honor paid to God by the creature.*

Adoration, praise and recollection

Praising God always involves remembering. We remember not only who God is, but what he has done. Anyone who begins to take seriously the call to praise will find that recollecting is one important element in the exercise.

Forgetting was one of Israel's great spiritual dangers. They were reminded over and over again during their wilderness wanderings of the deliverance God had wrought for them in leading them out of Egyptian slavery and through the Red Sea. Miracle after miracle attended them, and they were told to recall them often. Certain days and celebrations were given to help them remember.

When they finally arrived at the Jordan to cross over into the Promised Land, they were instructed to take twelve stones from the river bed and make of them a monument. When children in time to come would ask what those stones meant, they were to tell the story of the crossing of the Jordan River on dry ground. They were to be a people of remembrance. This would enable them to become the people they were called to be. Their worship would always involve recalling what great things the Lord had done for them.

We certainly can do no less. Our Lord Jesus Christ left us with two commands: "Love one another as I have loved you," and "Do this in remembrance of me." Remembering will always be a part of the praise we Christians offer to God. "When I survey the wondrous cross. . . ."

As we praise, that mercy and grace we meet at Calvary becomes personal for us. God's intervention in our lives, his saving presence, and daily help become additional reasons that we need to take time to praise him. It was the remembrance of the time when God's grace became vivid and real for him that prompts Watts to say:

> Sweet is the memory of thy grace,
>   My God, my heavenly King;
> Let age to age thy righteousness
>   In sounds of glory sing.

> How kind are thy compassions, Lord,
> How slow thine anger moves!
> But soon he sends his pardoning word,
> To cheer the soul he loves.
>
> Creatures, with all their endless race,
> Thy power and praise proclaim;
> But we, who taste thy richer grace
> Delight to bless thy name.

Praise: a gift and a weapon in our spiritual warfare.

"These meditations," says Watts, "are of great use in the beginning of our prayers, to abase us before the throne of God, to awaken our reverence, our dependence [on him], our faith, our hope, . . . and our joy [in him]."

Notice the words *reverence*, *dependence*, *faith*, *hope*, and *joy*. These we might call "by-products" of praise. They are God's gifts to us as we render him the praise we owe. It has often been said that we cannot out-give God. He is the great Giver, and one might reverently say that he will not allow himself to be "out-given." In one of the psalms he says to his people, "If I were hungry I would not tell you." He is jealous of his "god-ness" because that quality or essence is safe only with him.

Therefore, when we come to the work, the duty, the discipline of praise, we will take back more than we give. We can count on that. Its results in our lives will be more than commensurate with what we contribute. "Reverence and dependence" are qualities that frame our attitudes aright in relation to God. They are in no way demeaning of our human dignity, but they guard us against the sin of presumption as we approach the throne of the Most High.

"Faith, hope, and joy" are the positive gifts we carry away from the place of praise. Our outlook on life, which is so often marked by discouragement, perhaps even of bitterness, is sweetened and brightened when faith and hope shine in. In praise our hearts are opened to receive the truth of God's goodness. It is not by reasoning or argument, but by praise that the truth of his goodness will build the temple for his dwelling in our hearts.

In praise we join the eternal and unending praise that is already going on in heaven. In that sense, we *enter* heaven. The Orthodox Church symbolizes and visualizes this very effectively in its services, where each service is seen as joining the heavenly praise already going on. The sorrows of earth, and our own struggles and sorrows are but the background against which the glory of God's compassion shines. Praise opens our hearts to see this truth and encourages us in our spiritual pilgrimage. It lifts our spirits above the sordidness and darkness of the world, and it invites us to walk in the light we have seen and the hope we have encountered as we praise.

Do we see praise as a weapon against the darkness around us and the darkness within? Do we see that this weapon is offered to us by a kind and loving Father? If we did, I believe that we would be using it more faithfully and more effectively.

"These meditations are *of great use* as we begin our prayers, to humble us before the throne of God, to awaken our reverence, our dependence on him, our faith, our hope, and our joy in him."

It was the following hymn that John Wesley tried to sing when he lay dying. Three times he got out the first words, only to lose strength and fall back on his pillow.

> I'll praise my Maker while I've breath;
> And when my voice is lost in death,
>   Praise shall employ my nobler powers;
> My days of praise shall ne'er be past,
> While life, and thought, and being last,
>   Or immortality endures.

> Happy the man whose hopes rely
> On Israel's God; he made the sky,
>   And earth, and seas, and all their train.
> His truth for ever stands secure,
> He saves th'oppressed, he feeds the poor,
>   And none shall find his promise vain.

> The Lord pours eyesight on the blind;
> The Lord supports the fainting mind;
>   He sends the laboring conscience peace;
> He helps the stranger in distress,
> The widow and the fatherless,
>   And grants the prisoner sweet release.

> I'll praise him while he lends me breath;
> And when my voice is lost in death,
>   Praise shall employ my nobler powers;
> My days of praise shall ne'er be past
> While life, and thought, and being last,
>   Or immortality endures.

The Gift of Prayer

CHAPTER TWO

*H*aving already spoken of the nature of prayer and distinguished it into its several parts, I proceed to give some account of the gift or ability to pray. This holy skill of speaking to God in prayer hath been usually called a gift, and upon this account it hath been represented by the weakness and folly of some persons like the gift of miracles or prophecy which are entirely the effects of divine inspiration, wholly out of our reach and unattainable by our utmost endeavors. The malice of others hath hereupon taken occasion to reproach all pretenses to it as vain fancies and wild enthusiasm.

But I shall attempt to give so rational an account of it in the following sections, and lay down such plain directions how to attain it with the assistance of the Holy Spirit, and his blessing on our own diligence and labor, that I hope those prejudices will be taken off, and the unjust reproach be wiped away forever.

What the Gift of Prayer is

The gift of prayer may be thus described: it is an ability to suit our thoughts to all the various parts and designs of this duty and a readiness to express those thoughts before God in the fittest manner to profit our own souls and the souls of others that join with us. It is called a gift, partly because it was bestowed on the Apostles and primitive Christians in an immediate and extraordinary manner by the Spirit of God, and partly because there is the ordinary assistance of the Spirit of God required even to the attainment of this holy skill or ability to pray.

In the first propagation of the gospel it pleased the Spirit of God to bestow various powers and abilities on believers, and these were called the gifts of the Spirit (1 Corinthians 12:4, 8, 9). Such were the gifts of preaching, of exhortation, of psalmody—that is, of making and singing of psalms, of healing the sick, of speaking, several tongues, etc. Now, though these were given to men at once in an extraordinary way then, and the habits wrought in them by immediate divine power made them capable of exerting the several acts proper thereto on just occasions, yet these powers or abilities of speaking several tongues, of psalmody, of preaching and healing, are now to be obtained by human diligence, with due dependence on the concurring blessing of God. And the same must be said concerning the gift or faculty of prayer.

As the art of medicine or healing is founded on the knowledge of natural principles and made up of several rules drawn from the nature of things, from reason and observation, so the art of preaching is learned and attained by the knowledge of divine principles and the use of rules and directions for explaining and applying divine truths. And so the holy skill of prayer is built on a just knowledge of God and ourselves and may be taught in as rational a method by proper directions and rules. But because in a special manner we expect the aids of the Holy Spirit in things so serious and sacred, therefore the faculties of preaching and praying are called gifts of the Spirit even to this day, whereas that word is not nowadays applied to the art of medicine, or skill in the languages.

Forms of Prayer, of Free and Conceived Prayer, and Praying Extemporaneously

The gift of prayer is one of the noblest and most useful in the Christian life, and therefore to be sought with earnest desire and diligence. And in order to attain it, we must avoid these two extremes:

I. Confining ourselves entirely to precomposed forms of prayer.

II. An entire dependence on sudden motions and suggestions of thought.

I. The first extreme to be avoided is confining ourselves to set precomposed forms of prayer. I grant it lawful and convenient for weaker Christians to use a form of prayer rather than not perform that duty at all. Christ himself seems to have indulged it to his disciples in their infant state of Christianity (Luke 11:1, 2). I grant also that sometimes the most improved saints may find their own wants and desires and the frames of their own hearts so happily expressed in the words of other men, that they cannot find better, and may therefore in a very pious manner use the same, especially when they labor under a present deadness of spirit and great indisposition for the duty. It is also evident, that many assistances may be borrowed by younger and older Christians from forms of prayer well composed, without the use of the whole form as a prayer. And if I may have leave to speak the language of a judicious author that wrote more than forty years ago, I would say with him that forms may be useful and in some cases necessary: for,

1. "Some, even among Christians and professors, are so rude and ignorant, though it may be spoken to their shame, that they cannot tolerably express their desires in prayer; and must such utterly neglect the duty? Is it not better during their gross ignorance, to use the help of other's gifts and composures than not to pray at all? or to utter that which is senseless and impious? I speak it not to excuse their ignorance, or

that they should be encouraged to rest satisfied herein, but for the present necessity.

2. "Some again, though they can do it privately, and so far as may suffice in their secret addresses to God; yet when they are to pray before others lack either dexterity and fitness of expression, readiness of utterance, or confidence to use those abilities they have, whom yet I will not excuse from sinful bashfulness.

3. "It is possible that some bodily distemper, or sudden distraction, may befall such as are otherwise able, which may becloud their minds, weaken their memories, and dull their parts that they may be unfit to express themselves in extemporary conceptions. This may happen in case of melancholy, cold palsies, or the like distempers. I conclude then, that in the cases aforesaid, or the like, a form may be profitable and helpful. Nor is it a tying up of the Spirit, but if conscionably used, may be both attended with the Spirit's assistance, and find acceptance with God. Yet it will not hence follow that any should satisfy themselves in such stated and stinted forms: much less, that those who have praying abilities, should be enforced by others to rest in them. If ignorance, bashfulness, defect of memory, or other distemper, may render it excusable and necessary to some, is it fit all should rest in their measure? Where then will be that coveting earnestly the best gifts? Or why should those that are excellently gifted that way be hindered from the use and exercise of that gift, because others want it."

Thus far this worthy writer.

Now though the use of forms in such cases be not unlawful, yet a perpetual confinement to them will be attended with such inconveniences as these:

1. It much hinders the free exercise of our own thoughts and desires, which is the chief work and business of prayer, namely to express our desires to God. And whereas our thoughts and affections should direct our words, a set form of words directs our thoughts and affections. And while we bind ourselves to those words only, we damp our inward devotion and prevent the holy fire kindling within us. We discourage our active powers and passions from running out on divine subjects, and check the yearnings of our souls heaven-ward. The wise man tells us (Proverbs 14:10): "The heart knoweth his own bitterness; and a stranger doth not intermeddle with his joy." There are secret joys and unknown bitternesses which the holy soul longs to spread before God, and for which it cannot find any exact and correspondent expressions in the best of prayer books—now must such a Christian suppress all those thoughts and forbid himself all that sweet conversation with his God, because it is not written down in the appointed form?

2. The thoughts and affections of the heart that are truly pious and sincere are wrought in us by the Spirit of God, and if we deny them utterance because they are not found in prayer books, we run the danger of resisting the Holy Ghost, quenching the Holy Spirit, and fighting against the kind designs of God toward us, which we are so expressly cautioned against (1 Thessalonians 5:19), and which a humble Christian trembles to think of.

3. A confinement to forms cramps and imprisons those powers that God hath given us for improvement and use. It silences our natural abilities and forbids them to act, and it puts a bar upon our spiritual faculties and prevents their

growth. To satisfy ourselves with mere forms, to confine ourselves wholly to them and neglect to stir up and improve our own gifts, is one kind of spiritual sloth, and highly to be disapproved. It is hiding a talent in the earth, which God has given us on purpose to carry on a trade with heaven. It is an abuse of our knowledge of divine things to neglect the use of it in our converse with God. It is as if a man that had once used crutches to support him when he was feeble would always use them. Or because he has sometimes found his own thoughts happily expressed in conversation by another person, therefore he will assent to what that other person shall always speak and never speak his own thoughts himself.

4. It leads us into the danger of hypocrisy and mere lip service. Sometimes we shall be tempted to express those things which are not the very thoughts of our own souls, and so use words that are not suited to our present wants or sorrows or requests, because those words are put together and made ready beforehand.

5. The confinement of ourselves to a form, though it is not always attended with formality and indifference, yet it is very apt to make our spirits cold and flat, formal and indifferent in our devotion. The frequent repetition of the same words doth not always awaken the same affections in our hearts, which perhaps they were well suited to do when we first heard or made use of them. When we continually tread one constant road of sentences or track of expressions, they become like an old beaten path in which we daily travel, and we are ready to walk on without particular notice of the several parts of the way; so in our daily repetition of a form we neglect due attention to the full sense of the words. But there is something more suited to awaken the attention of the mind in a conceived prayer when a Christian is making his own way toward God, according to the present inclination of his soul and urgency of

his present wants. And to use the words of a writer lately cited, "While we are clothing the sense of our hearts in fit expressions, and as it were digging the matter of our prayers out of our own feelings and experience, it must needs keep the heart closer at work."

6. The duty of prayer is very useful to disclose to us the frame of our own spirits, but a constant use of forms will much hinder our knowledge of ourselves and prevent our acquaintance with our own hearts, which is one great spring of maintaining inward religion in the power of it. Daily observation of our own spirits would teach us what our needs are, and how to frame our prayers before God. But if we tie ourselves down to the same words always, our own observation of our hearts will be of little use since we must speak the same expressions, let our hearts be how they will. As therefore an inward search of our souls and intimate acquaintance with ourselves is a means to obtain the gift of prayer, so the exercise of the gift of prayer will promote this self-acquaintance, which is discouraged and hindered by the restraint of forms.

7. In the last place, I mention the most usual, most evident and convincing argument against perpetual confinement of ourselves to a form. And that is, because it renders our converse with God very imperfect. For it is not possible that forms of prayer should be composed that are perfectly suited to all our frames of spirit and fitted to all our occasions in the things of this life and the life to come. Our circumstances are always altering in this frail and mutable state. We have new sins to be confessed, new temptations and sorrows to be represented, new wants to be supplied. Every change of providence in the affairs of a nation, a family, or a person requires suitable petitions and acknowledgments. And all these can never be well provided for in any prescribed composition. I confess all our concerns of soul and body may be included in some large and

general words of a form which is no more suited to one time, or place, or condition, than to another. But generalities are cold and do not affect us, nor affect persons that join with us and whose case he that speaks in prayer should represent before God. It is much sweeter to our own souls and to our fellow worshipers to have our fears and doubts and complaints and temptations and sorrows represented in most exact and particular expressions, in such language as the soul itself feels when the words are spoken. Now, though we should often meet with precomposed prayers that are fitted to express our present case, yet the gift of prayer is as much better than any form as a general skill in the work of preaching is to be preferred to any precomposed sermons, as a perfect knowledge in the art of physic is better than any number of prescriptions, or as a prescription to make a medicine is preferable to one single medicine already made. But he that binds himself always to read printed sermons will not arrive at the art of preaching; and that man that deals only in prescriptions shall never become a skillful physician; nor can the gift of prayer be attained by everlasting confinement to forms.

Perhaps it may make stronger impressions on some persons, and go further toward the cure of their confinement to forms and their prejudices against the gift of prayer, to hear what a bishop of the Church of England has said on this matter:

"In the use of such prescribed forms to which a man hath been accustomed, he ought to be narrowly watchful over his own heart, for fear of that lip-service and formality, which in such cases we are more especially exposed to. For anyone so to set down and satisfy himself with his prayer-book, or some prescribed form, and to go no farther, this were still to remain in his infancy, and not to grow up in his new nature; this would be as if a man who had once need of crutches should always afterwards make use of them, and so necessitate himself to a continual impotency. Prayer by book is commonly of itself something flat and dead, floating for the most part too much in generalities, and not particular enough for each several occasion. There is not that life and vigor in it to engage the affections, as when it proceeds immediately from the soul itself, and is the natural expression of those particulars whereof we are most sensible. It is not easy to express what a vast difference a man may find, in respect of inward comfort and satisfaction, betwixt those private prayers that are thus conceived, and those prescribed forms which we say by rote, or read out of books."

(Bishop Wilkins, in his *Gift of Prayer*)

II. Another extreme to be avoided by all that would obtain the gift of prayer is a neglect of preparation for prayer, and an entire dependence on sudden motions and suggestions—as though we were to expect the perpetual impression of the Holy Spirit upon our minds like the Apostles and inspired saints, as though we had reason to hope for his continual impulses, both in the matter and words of prayer, without any forethought, or care, or premeditation of our own. It is true indeed that when a man hath premeditated the matter of his prayer and the method of it never so exactly, he ought not so to confine himself as to neglect or check any warm and pious desires that may arise in his heart in the midst of the duty. But this doth not hinder it being lawful and proper by all useful means to endeavor in general to learn the holy skill of praying, and to prepare also by meditation, or reading, or holy conversation, for the particular exercise of this gift and the performance of this duty.

Some persons imagine that if they use no form they must always pray extempore or without any premeditation, and are ready to think all free or conceived prayer is extempore; but these things ought to be distinguished. Conceived or free prayer is, when we have not the words of our prayer formed before hand, to direct our thoughts. But we conceive the matter or substance of our addresses to God first in our minds, and then put those conceptions in such words and expressions as we think most proper. And this may be done by some work of meditation before we begin to speak in prayer; partly with regard to the thoughts, and partly the expressions too. Extemporary prayer is when we, without any reflection or meditation beforehand, address ourselves to God and speak the thoughts of our hearts as fast as we conceive them. Now this is most properly done in that which is called ejaculatory prayer, when we lift up our souls to God in short yearnings of request or thanksgiving in the midst of any common affairs of life. But there may be some other occasions for it, namely:

I grant that in secret prayer, there is not the same degree of premeditation necessary as in public. For there a person takes a greater liberty to express his thoughts and the desires of his soul just as they rise within him, which may be very significant to awaken and maintain his own affections in that duty, though perhaps they would be very improper and disagreeable in public.

I grant also that persons of better natural parts, of a lively temper, or ready expression, of great heavenly-mindedness, or such as have been long exercised and experienced in this work, are not bound to premeditate all the materials and methods of their prayer in daily worship in a family. Nor are ministers, whose graces and talents have been well improved, obliged to think over all the substance of every public address to God beforehand. A short recollection of thought may supply such persons with matter for those constant returns of worship.

Nor are Christians who are possessed of such endowments bound at any time to an equal degree of premeditation as others are. Bishop Wilkins very pertinently tells us: "The proportion of gifts that a man hath received is the measure of his work and duty in this case." Yet upon some great and solemn occasions, public and private, when seasons are set apart for prayer, a regular premeditation is very useful and advantageous to persons of the highest attainments.

I grant further that there may be several calls of providence which may demand such sudden addresses to God, even from persons of less skill and experience—and they have then reason to hope for more especial assistance from the Spirit of God while they obey the call of present and necessary duty. But I am ready to suspect that some persons who are unskilled in praying, and yet cry out against premeditation, do indulge a degree of spiritual sloth that secretly prevails upon them, while they profess to be afraid of any thing that comes near to a form.

The arguments that may incline and encourage younger Christians to prepare their thoughts for prayer beforehand are these:

1. The common reason of man and light of nature teach us that *an affair of such solemnity and importance,* which requires our utmost care to perform it well, *cannot be done without some forethought.* The skill of a Christian in the inward exercise of grace is to be learned and improved by forethought and diligence—and much more in the external performance of a religious duty. Now if the light of nature leads us to it, and Scripture nowhere forbids, why should we not pursue the practice? The words of Scripture seem to encourage such premeditation, when it tells us we should not be rash with our mouth, nor let our heart be hasty to utter any thing before God (Ecclesiastes 5:2).

2. *That the heart should be prepared for prayer is certainly necessary.* The preparation of the heart is frequently spoken of in the word of God—now the heart cannot be prepared for any act of worship without some degree of premeditation. What is the use of reading the word of God just before prayer in our families? Why are we so often advised to recollect the sermons we hear when we retire for prayer, but that by premeditation we may be better fitted with materials for this duty?

3. *There can be no such thing as learning to pray in a regular way without it.* The distinction of the nature of prayer into its several parts—adoration, confession, petition—is all useless if we must not think beforehand. The excellent rules that ministers lay down to teach us to pray are mere trifling if we must not think beforehand. If we may not consider what our sins are, what our needs, and what our mercies before we speak in prayer, there is no possibility of ever learning to perform this part of Christian worship within any tolerable measure of decency or profit. An utter aversion to think beforehand, whatever the pretenses are, will be a most effectual bar against the attainment of the gift of prayer in any considerable degree.

4. *Due preparation for prayer is the way to serve God with our best.* But for younger Christians, unskilled in this work, to rush always into the presence of God in solemn prayer without due forethought even when there is time allowed for it, and to pour out words before God at all adventures, is no sign of that high reverence which they owe to so awful a majesty before whom angels veil their faces, who is jealous of his own worship, and abhors the sacrifices of fools.

If we utterly neglect preparation we shall be ready to fall into many inconveniences. Sometimes we shall be constrained to make long and indecent stops in prayer, not knowing what to say next. At other times we shall be in danger of saying those things that are very little to the purpose, and of wandering far from our purposed subject and design, which can never be acceptable to God. And sometimes when the mind is not regularly furnished, the natural spirits are put into a confused, incoherent, and impertinent rhapsody of words, whereby both God may be dishonored, and our own edification and the edification of others spoiled. While the Spirit of God stands afar off from us for a season, it may be on purpose, to reprove our negligence of a wise and holy care to learn to pray.

Some such unhappy practices as these in the last age, have given great offense to the pious and been a stumbling-block and scandal to the profane. The wicked and profane world have taken occasion from such practices to throw loads of reproach on all conceived prayer, under the name of praying extempore, and have endeavored to render all prayer, without books and forms, as odious as possible under this name. The more sober and pious part of the Church of England, that usually worship God by liturgies and precomposed forms, have been too ready to give ear to these reproaches and have, by this mean, been confirmed in their confinement to liturgies and prayer books. They have been hardened hereby against attempting to seek the gift of prayer themselves, and been tempted to oppose and censure those that have attained it. No small share of this public scandal will be found at the door of those few bold, ignorant, and careless men, who have been guilty of such rash and thoughtless addresses to God under a pretense of praying by the Spirit.

In opposition to this practice of premeditation, some pious and sincere Christian may say, "I have now and then meditated many things, which I desired to speak in prayer, but when I came to pray, I have found my thoughts enlarged beyond all my preparations, and carried away to dwell in prayer upon subjects and petitions of very different kind, and in a much more lively manner, to express my thoughts than I had before conceived." Now, I would persuade such a person to receive this divine assistance, not as an argument to neglect premeditation for the future, but as a reward of his diligence in preparing his heart beforehand for this work.

Another Christian will tell me that sometimes, when he has thought over many materials for his prayer before, he has found a greater confusion in his mind between his former preparations and his present suggestions than if he had prayed in an extemporary way.

In *reply* to this *objection*, I must confess that I have sometimes had the same unhappy experience—but I impute it to one of these three defects:

Either my *premeditation was very slight and imperfect*, as to the matter or method, so that I had not arranged the materials of my prayer in any settled form and order in my memory, but left them almost as much at uncertainty as new thoughts that might occur to my mind in praying. And it is more troublesome sometimes to mend and finish what is very imperfect, than to make entirely new.

Or, perhaps, my *premeditation had been chiefly the work of my head, without so due a consultation of the frame of my heart*. I had prepared my head but not my heart for prayer, and then it was no wonder that when the heart comes to be warmly engaged in praying, it runs far away from the mere premeditation of the head—and sometimes, betwixt both, created a confusion in the mind.

Or, it may be, my soul hath been out of frame and indisposed for prayer. And then I would not lay the fault upon premeditation, which would have been as bad or worse without it.

But where my preparation, both of head and heart, hath been carefully and wisely managed, I have had several experiences of the conveniency and usefulness of it, especially in my younger years, and upon some extraordinary and solemn occasions.

After all, if some particular persons have conscientiously and with due diligence attempted this way, and find they always pray more usefully and more honorably, with more regularity and delight, by the mere preparation of the heart for this duty, without fixing the parts and method of the prayer in their memory beforehand, they must follow those methods of devotion themselves which they have found most effectual to attain the best ends—but not forbid the use of premeditation to others whom God hath owned and approved in that way.

And let this be observed, that there are but a few Christians that attain so great a readiness and regularity in the gift of prayer without learning by premeditation. Far greater is the number of those whose performances are very crude for lack of thinking beforehand.

Having thus endeavored to secure you from these two dangerous extremes, namely a perpetual confinement to forms on the one hand, and a neglect of all premeditation on the other; I proceed.

In the gift of prayer, we are to consider these five things: The matter, the method, the expression, the voice, and the gesture. I shall treat of each of these at length.

The Matter of Prayer

First, it is necessary to furnish ourselves with proper matter, that we may be able to hold much converse with God; to entertain our souls and others agreeably and devoutly in worship; to assist the exercise of our own graces and others by a rich supply of divine thoughts and desires in prayer, that we may not be forced to make too long and indecent pauses whilst we are performing that duty; nor break off abruptly as soon as we have begun, for want of matter; nor pour out abundance of words to dress up narrow and scanty sense for want of variety of devout thoughts. I shall, therefore, first propose some rules in order to furnish ourselves with proper matter for prayer, and then lay down some directions concerning these materials of prayer, with which our souls are furnished.

Rules to furnish us with matter [for prayer] are these:

RULE 1. Labor after a large acquaintance with all things that belong to religion, for there is nothing that relates to religion but may properly make some part of the matter of prayer.

This is therefore the most general advice, and the most universal rule that can be given in this case—let us daily seek after a more extensive and more affecting knowledge of God and ourselves. A great acquaintance with God in his nature, in his persons, in his perfections, in his works, and in his word, will supply us with abundant furniture for invocation, adoration and praise, thanksgiving and blessing, and will suggest to us many arguments in pleading with God for mercy. An intimate acquaintance with ourselves and a lively sense of our own frames of spirit, our wants, our sorrows, and our joys, will also supply us with proper thoughts for confession, for petition, and for giving thanks. We should acquaint ourselves therefore with the word of God in a great degree, for it is there he reveals himself to us, and there he reveals us also to ourselves. Let the word of Christ dwell richly in you in all wisdom, that you may be furnished with petitions and praises.

We should also be watchful observers of the dealings of God with us in every ordinance and in every providence, and know well the state of our own souls. We should observe the working of our hearts toward God, or toward the creature, and call ourselves to account often, and often examine our temper and our life, both in our natural, our civil and religious actions. For this purpose, as well as upon many other accounts, it will be of great advantage to keep by us in writing some of the most remarkable providences of God and instances of his anger or mercy toward us, and some of our most remarkable carriages toward him, whether sins or duties or the exercises of grace. Such observations and remarks in our daily walking with God will be a growing treasury to furnish us for petition and praise. This seems to be the meaning of those Scriptures where we read of watching unto prayer (Ephesians 6:18, and 1 Peter 4:7). This will make us always ready to say something to God in prayer, both concerning him and concerning ourselves. Let our judgments be constantly well stored, and our graces and affections be lively, and lead us to the duty, and for the most part some proper matter will naturally arise and flow with ease and pleasure.

RULE 2. Let the nature of this duty of prayer, as divided into its several parts, be impressed upon your hearts and dwell in your memories.

Let us always remember that it contains in it these several parts of worship, namely, invocation, adoration, confession, petition, pleading, profession or self-resignation, thanksgiving, and blessing—which that we may retain the better in our minds, may be summed up in these four lines:

> Call upon God, adore, confess,
> Petition, plead, and then declare
> You are the Lord's, give thanks and bless,
> And let Amen confirm the prayer.

And by a recollection of these several parts of prayer, we may be assisted to go on step by step and to improve in the gift of performance of this part of worship. It would tend also to improve the gift of prayer if such persons as have time and capacity would set down all these parts of prayer as common places, and all the observable passages that occur in reading the Holy Scripture or other authors; or such passages as we hear delivered in prayer that are very affecting to our souls should be written down and registered under these headings. This would preserve such thoughts and expressions in our memories which have had a peculiar quickening influence upon us. Bishop Wilkins in his *Treatise on Prayer* has given us such collections of Scripture, and Mr. Henry, in a late book, has furnished us with a great many more, and judiciously ranged under their proper subjects.

RULE 3. Do not content yourselves merely with generalities, but if you would be furnished with larger supplies of matter, descend to particulars in your confessions, petitions, and thanksgivings.

Enter into a particular consideration of the attributes, the glories, the graces, and the relations of God. Express your sins, your wants and your sorrows with a particular sense of the mournful circumstances that attend them. It will enlarge your hearts with prayer and humiliation if you confess the aggravations that increase the guilt of your sins, namely whether they have been committed against knowledge, against the warnings of conscience, etc. It will furnish you with large matter for thankfulness if you run over the exalting and heightening circumstances of your mercies and comforts, namely that they are great, and spiritual, and eternal, as well as temporal, and that they were granted before you sought them, or as soon as you asked, etc. And let your petitions and your thanksgiving in a special manner be suited to the place and circumstances of yourselves, and those that you pray with, and those that you pray for. Our burdens, our cares, our wants, and sins are many; so are our mercies also, and our hopes, so are the attributes of our God, his promises and his graces. If we open our mouths wide, he will fill and satisfy us with good things, according to his word. If generalities were sufficient for us, one short form would make all others needless. It would be enough to express ourselves in this manner to God: "O Lord, thou art great and good, but we are vile sinners; give us all the mercies we stand in need of for time and for eternity, for the sake of Jesus Christ, and through him accept all our thanksgivings for whatsoever we have and hope for: to the Father, Son, and Holy Spirit be eternal glory. Amen." This is a most general and comprehensive prayer, and includes in it everything necessary. But no Christian can satisfy his soul, to go from day to day to the mercy seat and say nothing else but this. A saint in a right frame loves to pour out his soul before God in a hundred particulars. And God expects to see his children sensibly affected with their own special wants and his peculiar mercies, and to take notice of the lesser as well as of the more considerable circumstances of them. Let us not be constrained in ourselves then, for the hand of God and his heart are not constrained. Our Lord Jesus bids us ask, and promises it shall be given (Matthew 7:7). The Apostle Paul bids us in everything by prayer and supplication to make known our requests to God (Philippians 4:6). And the Apostle James tells us, we receive not because we ask not (James 4:2).

RULE 4. In order to furnish our minds with matter for prayer, it is very convenient at solemn seasons of worship to read some part of the word of God or some spiritual treatise written by holy men, or to converse with fellow Christians about divine things, or to spend some time in meditation of things that belong to religion.

This will not only supply us with divine matter but will compose our thoughts to a solemnity. Just before we engage in that work, we should be absent a little from the world that our spirits may be freer for converse with God. We may borrow matter for prayer from the word which we read, from inward reflections of our own souls, as well as from holy conferences. And many a saint hath found this true, that while he mused, the fire burned within him (Psalm 39:3), and while we speak to men about the affairs of religion and inward piety we shall certainly find something to say to God.

RULE 5. If we find our hearts, after all, very barren, and hardly know how to frame a prayer before God of ourselves, it has been oftentimes useful to take a book in our hand, wherein are contained some spiritual meditations in a petitionary form, some devout reflections, or excellent patterns of prayer; and above all, the Psalms of David, some of the Prophecies of Isaiah, some chapters in the Gospels, or any of the Epistles.

Thus we may lift up our hearts to God in secret in short requests, adorations or thanksgivings, according as the verses or paragraphs we read are suited to the case of our souls. This has obtained the name of mixed prayer, of which there is a further account under the fifth heading of the last chapter. This many Christians have experienced as a very agreeable help, and of great advantage in their secret retirement, that when they could not of themselves speak a prayer to God, they could yet interline what they read with holy yearnings toward God with fervent petitions, and by this means they have found their souls warmed, and oftentimes in the sight of God have performed this duty more agreeably in this method than other persons of a larger and more extensive gift with greater furniture of matter, and much fluency of language. Nor can I disapprove of what Bishop Wilkins says concerning secret prayer, namely, "That it is not always necessary here that a man should still keep on in a continual frame of speech, but in private devotions a man may take a greater freedom both for his phrase and matter. He may sometimes be at a stand and make a pause, there may be intermissions and blank spaces in respect of speech, wherein by meditation he may recover new matter to continue in this duty."

RULE 6. If you find your heart so very dry and unaffected with the things of religion that you can say nothing at all to God in prayer, that you have no divine matter occurs to your thoughts, go and fall down humbly before God, and tell him with a grievous complaint, that you can say nothing to him. Go and tell him that without his Spirit you cannot speak one expression, that without immediate assistances from his grace you cannot proceed in this worship. Tell him humbly that he must lose a morning or evening sacrifice, if he condescend not to send down fire from heaven upon the altar.

Plead with him earnestly for his own Spirit if it be but in the language of sighs and tears. Beg that he would never suffer your heart to be so hard, nor your soul to be so empty of divine things, that he would not only now but at all times furnish you for so glorious a work as this of converse with himself. And God knows the mind of his own Spirit, and he hears those groanings that cannot be uttered, and he understands their language, when the soul is as it were imprisoned and shut up that it cannot vent itself. Our heavenly Father hears the groans of the prisoner (Psalm 102:20). And there hath been glorious communion maintained with God before the end of that season of worship, when at the beginning of it the saint could say nothing else but, "Lord, I cannot pray."

Let it be noted here that when there is such a heaviness and deadness upon the spirit, such a coldness or distraction in this worship, and such an averseness and reluctance in the mind, it ought to be a matter of humiliation and deep self-abasement before God, especially when at any time we are sensible that it is owing to our own negligence or to some late guilt brought upon the conscience. Earnestly we should beg pardon for it, and as Bishop Wilkins says, "What we lack in the degrees of our duty, we should be sure to make up in humility, and this will be the most proper improvement of our failings, when we can strengthen ourselves by our very infirmities."

I proceed now to lay down some directions concerning the matter of our prayers, how to manage it right:

DIRECTION 1. Do not think it absolutely necessary to insist upon all the parts of prayer in every address to God, though in our stated and solemn prayers there are but few of them that can be well left out. What we omit at one time, we may perhaps pursue at another with more lively affection, that so we may fulfil all our errands at the throne of grace. But let us be sure to insist most upon those things which are warmest in our own hearts, especially in secret. And this is a good advice, even in social prayers, when those things we are deeply affected with are such as the company that joins with us may properly be concerned in too. Also let those parts of prayer have the largest share in the performance, for which our spirit is best prepared, and with which it is most sensibly impressed at the present season, whether it be adoration, petition, confession, or thanksgiving. This will not only furnish us with matter but will keep our spirits lively in the work, and will be the best means to affect those that join with us, and to call their graces into exercise. Those things indeed which our fellow worshipers cannot be concerned in are better laid aside till we come to speak to God alone.

DIRECTION 2. Suit the matter of your prayer to the special occasion of each particular duty, to the circumstances of the time, place and persons with and for whom you pray. This will be another spring of matter, and will direct you to the choice of proper thoughts and language for every part of prayer.

1. *The Time.* If it be morning, then we adore God as the watchful Shepherd of Israel, that slumbers not nor sleeps. Then we confess our inability to have defended ourselves through all the hours of darkness, while nature and our active powers lie as it were useless and dead. Then we give thanks to him that he hath secured us from the spirits of darkness, and given us rest in measure, and raised us in peace—"I laid me down and slept, with comfort, I awoke, for the Lord sustained me" (Psalm 3:5). Then we petition for divine counsel in all the affairs of the day, and the presence of God with us through all the cares, businesses, dangers, and duties of it.

In the evening we give thanks to God for all the mercies of the day, for which we offered our petitions in the morning. We confess the sins and follies of the day and humble our souls before God. We petition for proper mercies the succeeding night, with expressions of adoration, confession, and self-resignation, suited to the time—"I will lie me down in peace, O Lord, and sleep; for thou only makest me to dwell in safety" (Psalm 4:8).

Thus when we pray before or after a meal; on the Lord's Day, or our common days of business; in time of war or peace; in a season of public or private rejoicing; in a day of trouble or humiliation: let the several expressions of our prayer, in the various parts of it, be suited to the particular season.

2. *The Place, and the Persons.* If in our secret retirements, then we adore God in this language: "O Lord God, who seest in secret, who knowest the way that I take, thou hast commanded that thy children should ask thee in their closets, and thou hast promised to reward them openly." Here we ought to confess our more particular sins which the world knows not, and pour out our whole souls before God with great freedom and plainness. Tell him all our follies, our infirmities, our joys and sorrows; our brightest hopes, and our most gloomy and

dismal fears, and all the inward workings of our hearts, either toward himself or toward the creatures. Then we converse with God aright in prayer, when we, as it were, maintain a divine friendship with him in secret, and in our humble addresses hold correspondence with him as our heavenly and condescending Friend.

When we pray in a family the matter must be suited to the circumstances of the household, in confession of family sins, petitions and thanksgivings for family mercies—whether those with whom we live are sick or in health; whether they are in distress or in peace; whether fixed in their habitations, or removing: and our language to God ought to be suited to this variety of conditions.

In public worship or family devotions, where saints and sinners are present, a minister or a Christian that speaks in prayer should consider the circumstances of the whole congregation or family, and plead for suitable mercies.

But I think he should not be ashamed to express his faith and hope when he speaks to God, where there are many to join with him in that holy language, though every single hearer cannot heartily join and consent. Perhaps this may be a way to make unconverted persons that are present, blush and be ashamed, and be inwardly grieved; that they are forced to leave out many of the expressions of prayer used by ministers, and are convicted in themselves and confounded, because they cannot join in the same language of faith and hope, joy and thankfulness. For it is not necessary that every worshiper should lift up his soul to God according to every sentence spoken in social prayer, but only in such as are suited to his own case and state, and such as he can sincerely speak to God himself.

DIRECTION 3. Do not affect to pray long for the sake of length or to stretch out your matter by labor and toil of thought, beyond the furniture of your own spirit. God is not the more pleased with prayers merely because they are long, nor are Christians ever the more edified. It is much better to make up by the frequency of our devotions what we lack in the length of them, when we feel our spirits dry and our hearts constrained. We may also cry to God for the aids of his own Holy Spirit, even in the middle of our prayer, to carry us forward in that work. But every man is not fit to pray long. God has bestowed a variety of natural, as well as spiritual talents and gifts upon men. Nor is the best Christian, or a saint of the greatest gifts, always fit for long prayers—for hereby he may fall into many inconveniences.

The inconveniences of affected length in prayer are these:

1. Sometimes a person is betrayed by an affection of long prayers into crude, rash, and unseemly expressions in the presence of God, such as are unworthy of his divine Majesty and unbecoming our lowliness: sometimes he is forced into impertinent digressions and wanders away from the subject in hand, till his thoughts again recover themselves, and true spiritual worship is hereby hindered and corrupted. We shall rather therefore take the advice of Solomon upon this account: "Be not rash to utter anything before God; God is in heaven, and thou upon earth, therefore let thy words be few" (Ecclesiastes 5:2).

2. We are tempted hereby to tautologies, we say the same things over and over again, which our Saviour highly blames: "When ye pray, use not vain repetitions as the heathen do, for they think they shall be heard for their much speaking" (Matthew 6:7). Sometimes indeed in the midst of our warm affections in prayer, we are delightfully constrained in a repetition of the same words, through more fervency of spirit; and there are instances of it in Scripture; but for the most part our repetitions are such as evidence not the fervency, but the barrenness of our minds, and the slightness of our frame.

3. Again, we shall be in danger, through an affection of length, of tiring those that join with us—especially when a prayer is drawn out to many words with much dullness and deadness of spirit and without an agreeable variety of thought. I confess, when the Spirit is poured in plentiful degrees upon men, and upon some extraordinary occasions, persons have continued for an hour or two together, with a delightful variety of matter and expression, and instead of toil and labor to hold on they found it difficult to break off; their souls have been all the while near to God and they have held the attention of those that join with them, and kept their devotion warm. Our fathers have seen and felt it, but that spirit is much departed in our day. And there are seldom found amongst us any great lengths of prayer, with equal affection and devotion, maintained either in ourselves or others through so long a duty.

4. We are tempted also sometimes by this means to exceed the season that is allotted for us in prayer, especially where others are to succeed in the same work. Or else we intrench, it may be, upon other parts of worship that are to follow; hereby some of our fellow worshipers are made uneasy. And when persons are under a necessary engagement to be elsewhere by an appointed time, or else to be engaged in other duties, the latter part of their devotion is generally spoiled. It may be regarded here that even when Jacob wrestled with the angel he was required to let him go, for it was break of day (Genesis 32:26). As we must not make one duty to thrust out another, so neither should we manage any duty so as to make it a hard task to ourselves, or a toil to others, but a pleasure and spiritual entertainment to both.

While I am discouraging young Christians from that affectation of long prayers which arises from an ostentation of their parts, from a superstitious hope of pleasing God better by saying many words or from a trifling frame of spirit, I would not have my readers imagine that the shortest prayers are always the best. Our sinful natures are too ready to put off God in secret or in the family with a few minutes of worship, from mere sloth and weariness of holy things—which is equally to be blamed. For hereby we omit a great part of the necessary work of prayer in confessions, petitions, pleadings for mercy, or thanksgivings. Nor do I think that prayer in public assemblies should be so short as though the only design of it were a mere preface before the sermon or a benediction after it. Whereas social prayer is one considerable part, if not the chief duty of public worship, and we ought generally to continue so long in it as to run through the most necessary and important purposes of a social address to the Throne of Grace. Christian prudence will teach us to determine the length of our prayers agreeably to the occasion and present circumstances, and according to the measure of our own ability for this work.

The Method of Prayer

I proceed now to the second thing to be considered in the gift of prayer, and that is method. Method is necessary to guide our thoughts, to regulate our expressions, and dispose of the several parts of prayer in such an order as is most easy to be understood by those that join with us and most proper to excite and maintain our devotion and theirs. Though there is not a necessity of the same just and exact regularity here as in preaching the word, yet a well-regulated prayer is most agreeable to men, honorable in the sight of the world, and not at all the less pleasing to God. The Spirit of God, when he is poured out a spirit of prayer in the most glorious measures, doth not contradict the rules of a natural and reasonable method, although his methods may have infinite variety in them.

Some method must be used in order to secure us from confusion, that our thoughts may not be ill sorted or mingled and huddled together in a tumultuary and unseemly manner. This will be of use also to prevent tautologies or repetitions of the same thing, when each part of prayer is disposed into its proper place. This will guard us against roving digressions, when we have ranged our thoughts in order throughout every step of our prayer. Our judgment infers what sort of matter properly and naturally follows that which we are at present speaking, so that there is no need to fill up any empty spaces with matter that is not proper or not suited to the purpose. Those persons that profess to pray without observing any method at all, if they are very acceptable and affecting to others in their gift, do certainly use a secret and natural method, and proper connexions of one thing with another, though they themselves have not laid down any rule to themselves for it nor taken notice of the order of their own prayers.

The general rules of method in prayer which I would recommend to you are these three:

1. Let the general and particular headings in prayer be well distinguished, and usually let generalities be mentioned first, and particulars follow. As, for example, in adoration we acknowledge that God is all over-glorious in his nature, self-sufficient and all-sufficient, and we mention this with the deepest reverence and universal abasement of soul. And then we descend to praise him for his particular attributes of power, wisdom, goodness, etc., and exercise our particular graces accordingly. So in confession we first acknowledge ourselves vile sinners, corrupt by nature and of the same sinful mass with the rest of mankind, and then we confess our particular iniquities and our special guilt. So in our petitions we pray first for the churches of Christ all over the world and his interest

and his gospel throughout the earth, and then we petition for the churches in this nation, in this city, and that particular church of Christ to which we belong. Sometimes indeed there is a beauty also in summing up all the particulars at last in one generality; as when we have praised God for his several perfections to the utmost of our capacity, we cry out, "Lord, thou art exalted above all our praises; thou art altogether great and glorious." Or, when we have confessed several particular sins, we fall down before God as persons that are all over defiled and guilty. When we have petitioned for particular mercies, we then ask that God who is able to do for us above what we can ask or think, that he would bestow all other comforts and every blessing that he knows needful for us. But still this rule must be observed, that general and particular headings ought to be so distinguished, as to make our method of prayer natural and agreeable.

2. Let things of the same kind, for the most part, be put together in prayer. We should not run from one part to another by starts and sudden wild thoughts, and then return often to the same part again, going backward and forward in confusion. This bewilders the mind of him that prays, disgusts our fellow worshipers, and injures their devotion. This will lead us into vain repetitions, and we shall lose ourselves in the work. Yet I would give this limitation, that sometimes the same matter may come in naturally, under two or three parts of prayer, and be properly disposed of in two or three places by a judicious worshiper. As the mention of some of the attributes of God under the heading of adoration, where we praise him for his own perfections, and under the heading of pleading for mercy, when we use his power, his wisdom, or his goodness as an argument to enforce our petitions. And under the heading of thanksgiving also, when we bless him for the benefits that proceed from his goodness, his power, or his wisdom. So in the

beginning of a prayer in our invocation of God, we put in a sentence or two of confession of our unworthiness and of petition for divine assistance. So toward the conclusion of prayer it is not amiss to use a sentence or two consisting of such matter as may leave a suitable impression upon our minds, though perhaps something of the same matter may have been before mentioned, as, to ask forgiveness of all the imperfections of our holy things; to entreat that God would hear all our requests in the name of our Lord Jesus; to recommend our prayers into the hands of our Redeemer, our great High-Priest; and to commit our whole selves to the conduct of divine grace till we are brought safe to glory. But then all this must be done with such a variety of expression and with some proper connexions, as will render it agreeable in itself, and will entertain the minds of those that join with us, and give them delight rather than hinder their devotion.

3. Let those things, in every part of prayer, which are the proper objects of our judgment, be first mentioned, and then those that influence and move our affections. Not that we should follow such a manner of prayer as is more like preaching, as some imprudently have done, speaking many divine truths without the form or air of prayer. It is a very improper custom, which some persons have taken up and indulged, when divine truths come to be mentioned in prayer, that they run great lengths in a doctrinal way. Yet there is occasion frequently in prayer, under the several parts of it, for the recollecting of divine truths, and these lay a proper foundation for warm and tender expressions to follow. As, "O Lord, thou art good, and thou dost good; why should I continue so long without partaking of thy goodness? My sins arc great, and my iniquities have many aggravations; O that I might mourn for them before thee in secret! O that I could pour out my soul before thee in sorrow, because of my multiplied offenses!"

Thus let the language of affection follow the language of our judgment, for this is the most rational and natural method.

Having laid down these general rules, the best particular method I can direct you to is that division of the parts of prayer mentioned in the foregoing chapter. I know not a more natural order of things than this is. To begin with invocation, or calling upon God, then proceed to adore that God whom we invoke, because of his various glories, we are then naturally led to the work of confession—considering what little contemptible creatures we are in the presence of so adorable a God—and to humble ourselves, because of our abounding sins and our many necessities. When we have given praise to a God of such holiness, and having spread our wants before God, petitions for mercy naturally follow, and pleading with such divine arguments as the Spirit and the word of God put into our mouths should accompany our requests. After all, we resign ourselves into the hands of God and express our self-dedication to him. Then we recollect the mercies we have received, and out of gratitude pay him our tribute of honor and thanks. And as he is glorious in himself and glorious in his works of power and grace, so we bless him and ascribe everlasting glory to him. I cannot but think it is a very useful thing for young beginners in the work of prayer to remember all these headings in their order, to dispose of their thoughts and desires before God in this method, proceeding regularly from one part to another. And as this must needs be useful to assist and teach us to pray in public, so sometimes in our secret retirements it may not be improper to pursue the same practice.

Yet it must be granted there is no necessity of confining ourselves to this or to any other set method, no more than there is of confining ourselves to a form in prayer. Sometimes the mind is so divinely full of one particular part of prayer, perhaps of thanksgiving, or of self-resignation, that high expressions of gratitude and of devoting ourselves to God break out first.

"Lord, I am come to devote myself to thee in an everlasting covenant. I am thine, through thy grace; and through thy grace I will be thine forever." Or thus: "Blessed be thy name, O Lord God Almighty, for thine abundant benefits, that fill my soul with the sense of them. For thou hast pardoned all my iniquities and healed all my diseases."

Sometimes even in the beginning of a prayer, when we are insisting on one of the first parts of it, we receive a divine hint from the Spirit of God that carries away our thoughts and our whole souls with warm affection into another part that is of a very different kind, and that usually perhaps comes in near the conclusion. And when the Spirit of God thus leads us, and our souls are in a very devout frame, we are not to quench the Spirit of God in order to tie ourselves to any set rules or prescribed method.

There is no necessity that persons of great talents, of divine affections, of much converse with God, and that have attained to a good degree of this gift by long exercise, should bind themselves to any one certain *method* of prayer. For we find the prayers recorded in holy Scripture are very various in the order and disposition of them, as the Spirit of God and the divine affections of those saints led and guided them. But still there is some method observed, and may be traced and demonstrated.

I am persuaded that if young Christians did not give themselves up in their first essays of prayer to a loose and negligent habit of speaking everything that comes uppermost, but attempted to learn this holy skill by a recollection of the several parts of prayer, and disposing their thoughts into this method, there would be great numbers in our churches that would have arrived at a good degree of the gift of prayer and be capable afterwards of giving a more glorious and unbounded loose to their souls, without breaking the rules of just and natural method—and that to the great edification of our churches as well as of their own families.

Expression in Prayer

The third thing that relates to the gift of prayer is expression. Though prayer be the proper work of the heart, yet in this present state, in secret as well as in social prayer, the language of the lips is an excellent aid in this part of worship. A person indeed may pray heartily and effectually, and yet make use of no words: sometimes the desires of the heart may be too big to be expressed, when the Spirit of God is with us in plentiful operations and assists us to plead with sighs and groans which cannot be uttered (Romans 8:26). Persons that are dumb may think over their wants and raise their souls to God in longing desires and wishes for grace in a time of need. Nor is there any necessity of using language upon God's account, for he knows the desires of our hearts and our secret yearnings toward him. He that hears without ears understands us without words. Yet as language is of absolute necessity in social prayer, that others may join with us in our addresses to God, so for the most part we find it necessary in secret too, for there are few persons of so steady and fixed a power of meditation as to maintain their devotion warm and to converse with God, or with themselves profitably, without words.

Here I shall first lay down some directions how to attain a rich treasure of expression in prayer. And secondly, give several rules about the choice and use of words and expressions. The directions to attain a treasury of expressions are these:

DIRECTION 1. Besides the general acquaintance with God and yourselves that was prescribed under a former heading, labor after the fresh, particular, and lively sense of the greatness and grace of God, and of your own wants, and sins, and mercies, whenever you come to pray. This will furnish you with abundance of proper expressions. The passions of the mind, when they are moved, do mightily help the tongue. They fill the mouth with arguments. They give a natural eloquence to those who know not any rules of art, and they almost constrain the dumb to speak. There is a remarkable instance of this in ancient history, when Atys the son of Croesus, who was dumb from his childhood, saw his father ready to be slain, the violence of his passion broke the bonds wherewith his tongue was tied and he cried out to save him. Beggars that have a pinching sense of hunger and cold find out variety of expressions to tell us their needs and to plead for relief. Let our spiritual senses therefore be always awake and lively, and our affections always warm, and lead the duty, then words will follow in a greater or less degree.

DIRECTION 2. Treasure up such expressions especially as you read in Scripture, and such as you have found in other books of devotion, or such as you have heard fellow Christians make use of, whereby your own hearts have been sensibly moved and warmed. Those forms of speaking that have had great influence and success upon our affections at one time, may probably have a like effect also at other seasons, if so be we take care not to confine ourselves to them constantly, lest formality and thoughtlessness should grow thereby.

Though the limitation of ourselves to a constant set form of words be justly disapproved, yet there is great use of serious, pious, and well-composed patterns of prayer in order to form our expressions and furnish us with proper praying language. And I wish the assistances that might be borrowed thence were not so superstitiously abandoned by some persons as they are idolized by others. But I suppose no persons will disapprove the advice if I desire them to remember the more affectionate sentences in the psalms of David, and the complaints of Job and other holy men, when they breathe out their souls to God in worship. These in a nearer and more particular sense may be called the words which the Holy Spirit teacheth; and whenever they suit our circumstances, they will always be pleasing to God. Besides, they are such as Christians are most acquainted with, and pious souls are most affected with them. The Spirit of God in praying and preaching will often bless the use of his own language. And I am persuaded this is one way whereby the Spirit helps our infirmities and becomes a Spirit of supplication in us, by suggesting to us particular passages of Scripture that are useful to furnish us both with matter and expression in prayer.

The most authentic judge of fine thoughts and language that our age has produced assures us of the beauty and glory of the style of Scripture, and particularly in this respect, that it is most proper to teach us how to pray. I cannot forbear transcribing this paragraph from the *Spectator*, 14th June 1712:

"It happens very well that the Hebrew idioms run into the English tongue with a peculiar grace and beauty: our language has received innumerable elegancies and improvements from that infusion of Hebraisms, which are derived to it out of the poetical passages of holy writ; they give a force and energy to our expressions, warm and animate our language, and convey our thoughts in more ardent and intent phrases than any that are to be met with in our own tongue; there is something so pathetic in this kind of diction, that it often sets the mind in a flame, and makes our hearts burn within us. How cold and dead doth a prayer appear that is composed in the most elegant and polite forms of speech which are natural to our tongue, when it is not heightened by that solemnity of phrase which may be drawn from the sacred writings? It has been said by some of the ancients that if the gods were to talk with men they would certainly speak in Plato's style; but I think we may say with justice, that when mortals converse with their Creator they cannot do it in so proper a style as that of the holy Scripture."

It would be of excellent use to improve us in the gift of prayer, if in our daily reading the word of God we did observe what expressions were suited to the several parts of this duty; adoration, confession, petition, or thanksgiving. And let them be wrought into our addresses to God that day. Nay, if we did but remember one verse every day, and fix it into our hearts by frequent meditation, and work it into our prayers morning and evening, it would in time grow up to a treasure of divine sense and language, fit to address our Maker upon all occurrences of life. And it has been observed that persons of lesser capacity and no learning have attained to a good measure of this holy skill of prayer merely by having their minds well furnished with words of Scripture, and have been able to pour out their hearts before God in a fluency of proper thoughts and language, to the shame of those that have been blessed with brighter parts and have enjoyed the advantage of a learned education.

Yet I would lay down two cautions about the use of Scripture language.

One is that we should not affect too much to impose an allusive sense upon the words of Scripture, nor use them in our prayers in a signification very different from the true meaning of them. Not that I would utterly disallow and condemn all such allusive expressions—as for instance, that which is frequently used when we desire mercies for our souls and bodies, to ask the blessings of the upper and the nether springs. There may be some such phrases used pertinently enough. The commonness of them also makes them something more agreeable. Yet if we affect to show our wit or ingenuity by seeking pretty phrases of Scripture and using them in an allusive sense, very foreign to the original purpose of them, we shall be in danger of leading ourselves into many mistakes in the interpretation of Scripture, and expose ourselves sometimes to the peril of mistaking the true sense of a text, by having frequently fixed a false meaning upon it in our prayers.

Another caution in using Scripture language is this, that we abstain from all those expressions which are of a very dubious sense and hard to be understood. If we indulge the use of such dark sentences in our speaking to God, we might as well pray in an unknown tongue, which is so much disapproved by the Apostle (1 Corinthians 14:9, 14). Let not therefore the pomp and sound of any hard Hebrew names or obscure phrases in Scripture allure us to be fond of them in social prayer, even though we ourselves should know the meaning of them, lest we confound the thoughts of our fellow worshipers.

DIRECTION 3. Be always ready to engage in holy conference and divine discourse. This will teach us to speak of the things of God. Let it be your delightful practice to recollect and talk over with one another the sermons you have heard, the books of divinity you have been conversant with, those parts of the word of God you have lately read, and especially your own experiences of divine things. Hereby you will get a large treasure of language to clothe your pious thoughts and affections.

It is a most profitable practice, after you have heard a sermon, to confer with some fellow Christian that heard it too, and run over all the particulars of it that you can retain in your memory. Then retire and pray them over again, that is, make them the matter and substance of your address to God. Plead with him to instruct you in the truths that were mentioned, to incline you to perform the duties recommended, to mourn over and mortify the sins that were reproved, to teach you to trust and live upon the promises and comforts proposed, and to wait and hope for the glories revealed in that sermon. Let this be done frequently afterwards, in the same week, if the sermon be suited to your case and condition of soul. This will furnish you incredibly with riches of matter and expression for the great duty of prayer.

The reason why we lack expression in prayer is, many times, because we accustom ourselves so little to speak about the things of religion, and another world. A man that hath but a tolerable share of natural parts, and no great volubility of speech, learns to talk well upon the affairs of his own trade and business in the world, and scarce ever wants words to discourse with his dealers. And the reason is because his heart and his tongue are frequently engaged therein. Thus, if our affections are kept warm and we accustom ourselves frequently to speak of the things of religion to men, we shall learn to express ourselves better about the same divine concerns when we come before God.

DIRECTION 4. Pray earnestly for the gift of utterance and seek the blessing of the Spirit of God upon the use of proper means to obtain a treasure of expressions for prayer. The great apostle prays often for a freedom of speech and utterance in his ministry, "that he may speak the mystery of Christ, and make it manifest so as he ought to speak" Col. 4:4. So the gift of utterance in prayer is a very fit request to be made to God for the advantage of our own souls and those that join with us. The wise man tells us, in Prov. 16:1, "That the preparation of the heart in man, and the answer of the tongue is from the Lord." Let us pray then, that when God hath prepared our heart for his worship, he would also teach our tongue to answer the thoughts and desires of the heart and to express them in words suitable and answering to all our inward spiritual affections. A happy variety of expression and holy oratory in prayer, is one of these "good and perfect gifts that come down from above, from God, the Father of lights and knowledge" James 1:17.

The rules about the choice and use of proper expressions in prayer are these:

RULE 1. Choose those expressions that best suit your meaning, that most exactly answer the ideas of your mind and are fitted to your sense and apprehension of things. For the design of prayer is to tell God the inward thoughts of your heart. If you speak therefore what is not in the heart, though the words be ever so fine and tender, it is but a mere mockery of God. Let your tongues be the true interpreters of your minds. When our souls are filled with a lively impression of some of the attributes or works of God, when our hearts are overpowered with a sense of our own guilt and unworthiness or big with some important request, O what a blessed pleasure it is to hit upon a happy expression that speaks our very soul and fulfils all our meaning, and what a pleasure doth it convey to all that join with us, who have their spiritual senses exercised! and it helps to excite in them the same devotion that dictated to us the words we speak—the royal preacher, in Eccl. 12:10, "Sought out and gave good heed to find, and to set in order acceptable words" in his sermons, that they might be "as goads and nails fastened by the master of assemblies." That is, that they might leave a strong and lasting impression on those that hear; that by piercing deep into the heart as goads, they might be fixed as nails. And there is the same reason for the choice of proper words in prayer.

RULE 2. Use such a way of speaking as may be most natural and easy to be understood and most agreeable to those that join with you. The apostle gives this direction to the Corinthians, concerning their public worship: "Except ye utter by the tongue words easy to be understood, how shall it be known what is spoken? for you shall speak into the air" 1 Cor. 16: 9. Avoid, therefore, all foreign and uncommon words which are borrowed from other languages and not sufficiently naturalized, or which are old and worn out of use. Avoid those expressions which are too philosophical, and those which savor too much of mystical divinity. Avoid a long train of dark metaphors or of expressions that are used only by some particular violent party men. Avoid length and obscurity in your sentences and in the placing of your words, and not interline your expressions with too many parenthesis, which cloud and entangle the sense.

And here I beg leave to give one or two instances of each of these improper methods of speaking. Not that I ever heard these very phrases used by any ministers or private Christians in prayer. But, as vices of the life are rendered most hateful, and are best cured or prevented by seeing them represented in their plainest and most odious colors, so the vices of speech and improprieties of expression are best avoided by a plain representation of them in their own complete deformity. This will deter us from coming near them, and make us watchful against all those forms of speaking that border upon these follies. And indeed, without giving examples of each of these faults, I know not how to make the unlearned Christian understand the things he ought to avoid.

By uncommon words I mean such as are either too new or too old for common use.

Old and obsolete words are such as these: *we do thee to wit*, for *we acquaint thee*; *leasing*, for *lying*; a *gin*, for a *snare*. Some such words as these yet stand in our translation of the Bible. Many of these you may find in the old translation of the Psalms, in the Common Prayer book, and in the meter of Hopkins and Strenhold—which might be proper in the age when they were written but are now grown into contempt.

New words are, for the most part, borrowed from foreign languages, and should not be used in social prayer till they are grown so common that there appears no difficulty to the hearers, nor affectation in the speaker. Such as these, which have a French original: *Thou, O Lord, art our dernier resort*; i.e., our last refuge. *The whole world is but one great machine, managed by thy puissance*; i.e. an engine managed by thy power. *We are chagrined because of the hurries and temptations of the malign spirit*; i.e. we are vexed and grown uneasy by reasons of the temptations of the devil. Or these, which are borrowed from the Latin: "The beatific splendors of thy face erradiate the celestial region and felicitate the saints: there are the most exuberant profusions of thy grace, and the sempiternal efflux of thy glory."

By *Philosophical* expressions, I intend such as are taught in the academical schools in order to give learned men a shorter and more comprehensive knowledge of things, or to distinguish nicely between ideas that are in danger of being mistaken without such distinction. As for example, it is not proper to say to God in public prayer—"Thou art hypostatically three and essentially one. By the plentitude and perfection in thine essence, thou art self-sufficient for thine own existence and beatitude; who in an incomplex manner eminently, though not formally, includest all the infinite variety of complex ideas that are found among the creatures." Such language as this may be indulged perhaps in secret by a man that is accustomed to meditate under these forms; but his less informed fellow-Christian would no more be edified by them than by praying in an unknown tongue.

By the language of *mystical divinity*, I mean such incomprehensible sort of phrases as a sect of divines among the Papists have used, and some few Protestants too nearly imitated. Such are, ". . . of the deform fund of the soul, the superessential life, of singing a hymn in silence; that God is an abyss of light, a circle whose center is everywhere, and his circumference nowhere; that hell is the dark world made up of spiritual sulphur, and other ingredients not united or harmonized, and without that pure balsamic oil that flows from the heart of God." These are great swelling words of vanity that captivate silly people into raptures by the mere sound without sense.

By running *long metaphors*, I mean the pursuing of similitude or metaphor, and straining so far as to injure the doctrines of religion by a false meaning or very improper expressions. Such was the language of the foolish writer who bids us "give our hearts to the Lord, cut them with the knife of contrition, take out the blood of your sins by confession, afterwards wash it with sanctification," etc.

By sentences that savor too much of *party-zeal*, I mean such as would be useless if not offensive to Christians of different judgments, that join with us in prayer. We should not in our prayers too much insist on the corruptions of doctrine and worship in any church when some of that communion join with us, nor of the infant's interest in the covenant of grace and baptism the first seal of it, when Baptists are worshiping with us together. Our prayers should not savor of anger and uncharitableness, for we are bid "to lift up holy hands without wrath" 1 Tim. 2: 8.

When I recommend such expressions as are easy to be understood, it is evident that you should avoid *long and entan-*

gled sentences, and place your thoughts and words in such an order as the heart of the hearers may be able to receive and join in the worship, as fast as their ears receive the words. As in all our conversations and conferences and discourses, we should labor to make everything we say to be understood immediately. So especially in prayer where the affections should be moved, which cannot well be done if the judgment must take much pains to understand the meaning of what is said.

RULE 3. *Let your language be grave and decent—which is a medium between magnificence and crudeness.* Let it be plain, but not coarse. Let it be clean, but not at all lofty and glittering. Job speaks of "choosing his words to reason with God," Job 9:14. Some words are choice and beautiful, others are unseemly and disagreeable. Beware of all wild, irregular, and vain expressions that are unsuited to so solemn a part of worship. The best direction I can give you in this case is to make use of such language as you generally use in your serious discourses upon religious subjects, when you confer with one another about the things of God. For then the mind is composed to gravity, and the tongue should answer and interpret the mind. The language of a Christian in prayer is the clothing of his thoughts or the dress of his body—decent and neat, but not pompous nor gaudy; simple and plain, but not careless, uncleanly, or rude.

Avoid, therefore, *glittering language* and *affected style.* When you address God in worship, it is a fault to be ever borrowing phrases from the theater and profane poets. This does not seem to be the language of Canaan. Many of their expressions are too light and wild and airy for so awful a duty. An excessive fondness of elegance and finery of style in prayer reveals the same pride and vanity of mind as an affectation of many jewels and fine apparel in the house of God. It betrays us into neglect of our hearts, and of experimental religion, by an affectation to make the nicest speech and say the finest things we can, instead of sincere devotion and praying in the spirit. Besides, if we will deal in lofty phrases, Scripture itself sufficiently abounds with them; and these are the most agreeable to God and most affecting to his own people.

Avoid *crude* and *coarse* and too *familiar expressions*, such as excite any contemptible or ridiculous ideas, and such as raise any improper or irregular thoughts in the mind, or base and improper images—for these much injure the devotion of our fellow-worshipers. And it is very culpable negligence to speak to God in such a rude and unseemly manner as would ill become us in the presence of our fellow-creatures when we address ourselves to them. Not but that God hears the language of the lowliest soul in secret, though he is not capable of expressing himself with all the decencies that are to be desired. Yet it is certain that we ought to seek to furnish ourselves with comely methods of expression, that so our performance of this duty may be rendered pleasing to those with whom we worship. And there is no necessity for being rough and slovenly in order to be sincere. Some have been guilty of great indecencies, and exposed religion to profane scoffs, by a too familiar mention of the name of Christ, and by irreverent freedoms when they speak to God. I cannot approve of the phrases of "rolling upon Christ," of "swimming upon Christ to dry land," of "taking a lease of Christ for all eternity." I think we may fulfil that command of coming boldly to the throne of grace without such language that can hardly be justified from rudeness and immodesty. Persons are sometimes in danger of indecencies in borrowing *crude and trivial or uncleanly similitudes*: they *rake all the sins of loathsomeness* to fetch metaphors for their sins, and praying for the coming of Christ; they *fold up the heavens like an old cloak*, and *shovel days out of the way.*

By these few instances you may learn what to avoid. And remember that words as well as things grow old and uncomely, and some expressions that might appear decent threescore years ago, would be highly improper and offensive to the ears of the present age. It is, therefore, no sufficient apology for these phrases, that men of great learning and most eminent piety have made use of them.

RULE 4. *Seek after those ways of expression that are tender and sensitive, such as denote the fervency of affection and carry life and spirit with them,* such as may awaken and exercise our love, our hope, our holy joy, our sorrow, our fear, and our faith, as well as express the activity of those graces. This is the way to raise, assist, and maintain devotion. We should therefore avoid such a sort of style as looks more like preaching, which some persons that affect long prayers have been guilty of to a great degree. They have been speaking to the people and teaching them the doctrines of religion and the mind and will of God, rather than speaking to God the desires of their own minds. They have wandered away from God to preach to men. But this is quite contrary to the nature of prayer. For prayer is our own address to God, declaring our sense of divine things and pouring out our hearts before him with warm and proper affections. And there are several modes of expression that promote this end. As,

1. *Exclamations*, which serve to set forth an affectionate wonder, a sudden surprise, or violent impression of any thing on the mind. "O how great is thy goodness, which thou hast laid up for them that fear thee!" Ps. 81:19. "How precious are thy thoughts to me, O God; how great is the sum of them!" Ps. 139:17. "O wretched man that I am! who shall deliver me?" Rom. 7: 24.

2. *Interrogations*, when the plain sense of any thing we declare unto God is turned into a question, to make it more

emphatic and affecting. "Whither shall I go from thy Spirit? Whither shall I flee from thy presence?—Do I not hate them that hate thee?" Ps. 139:7, 21. "Who shall deliver me from the body of this death?" Rom. 7:24.

3. *Appeals to God*, concerning our own wants or sorrows, our sincere and deep sense of the things we speak to him. "Lord, thou knowest all things; thou knowest that I love thee" John 21:17. So David appeals to God, Ps. 69:5. "My sins are not hid from thee" Ps. 56:8. "Thou tellest all our travels, or our wanderings; are not my tears in thy book?" Job 10:7. Thou knowest that I am not wicked: my witness is in heaven, and my record is on high" Job 16:19.

4. *Expostulations*, which are indeed one particular sort of interrogations, and are fit to express not only deep dejections of the mind, but to enforce any argument that is used in pleading with God, either for mercy for his saints, or the destruction of his enemies. "Look down from heaven, behold from the habitation of thy holiness and of thy glory, where is thy zeal and thy strength? The sounding of thy bowels and thy mercies towards me, are they restrained? O Lord, why hast thou made us to err from thy ways, and hardened our hearts from thy fear?" Isa. 62:15, 17. "Awake, awake, put on strength, O arm of the Lord: Art not thou it that hath cut Rahab and wounded the dragon? Art thou not it that hath dried the sea, the waters of the great deep?" Isa. 51: 9, 10. "Will the Lord cast off forever, and will he be favorable no more?" Ps. 77:8. "O Lord God of hosts, how long wilt thou be angry?" Ps. 80:4. "Wherefore hidest thou thy face, and forgettest our affliction?" Ps. 64:24. God invites his people thus to argue with him. "Come, now, let us reason together, saith the Lord" Isa. 1:18. And holy men, in humble and reverend expostulations, have with many reasons, pleaded their cause before God; and their words are recorded as our patterns.

5. *Options* or *wishes*, fit to set forth serious and earnest desires. "O that I might have my request!" Job 6:8. "O that my ways were directed to keep thy statutes!" Ps. 119:5.

6. *Apostrophes*; that is, when in the midst of our addresses to God, we turn off the speech abruptly to our own souls, being led by the vehemence of some sudden devout thought. So David, in the beginning of Psalm 16. "Preserve me, O God; for in thee do I put my trust. O my soul, thou hast said to the Lord, thou art my Lord," etc. In meditations, psalms, hymns or other devotional compositions, these *apostrophes* may be longer and more frequent. But in prayer they should be very short, except when the speech is turned from one person of the blessed Trinity to another. Thus: "Great God, hast thou not promised that thy Son shall have the heathen for his inheritance and that he should rule the nations? Blessed Jesus, how long ere thou assumest this kingdom? When wilt thou send thy Spirit to enlighten and convert the world? When, O eternal Spirit, wilt thou come and shed abroad thy light and thy grace through all the earth?"

7. *Ingeminations*, or redoubling our expressions, which argue an eager and inflamed affection: "O Lord God, to whom vengeance belongeth, show thyself" Ps. 94:1, 2. "My soul waits for the Lord more than they that watch for the morning; I say, more than they that watch for the morning" Ps. 130:6. And the conclusion of Psalm 72 is, "Blessed be the Lord forevermore, amen, and amen." But here let us take care to distinguish between those repetitions that arise from real fervency of spirit and those that are used merely to lengthen out a prayer, or that arise from mere barrenness of heart, the want of matter. It is far better, at least in public prayer, to yield to our present indisposition and shorten the duty, than to fill up our time with constant repetitions such as, "O Lord, our God, if it be thy blessed will, we entreat thee, we beseech

thee, O Lord, have mercy upon us." For though some of these expressions may be properly enough repeated several times in a prayer, yet filling up every empty space by stretching out almost every sentence with them, is not agreeable to our fellow-worshipers, nor an ornament, nor a help to our devotion or theirs.

RULE 5. *Do not always confine yourselves to one set form of words to express any particular request, nor take too much pains to avoid an expression merely because you have used it in prayer heretofore.* Be not over fond of a nice uniformity of words nor of perpetual diversity of expression in every prayer. It is best to keep the middle between these two extremes. We should seek indeed to be furnished with a rich variety of holy language, that our prayers may always have something new and something entertaining in them, and not tie ourselves to express one thing always in one set of words, lest this make us grow formal and dull, and indifferent in those petitions. But on the other hand, if we are guilty of a perpetual affectation of new words which we never before used, we shall sometimes miss our own best and most spiritual meanings and many times be driven to great impropriety of speech. And at best, our prayers by this mean will look like the fruit of our fancy and invention and labor of the head, more than the yearnings of the heart. The imitation of those Christians and ministers that have the best gifts will be an excellent direction in this, as well as the former cases.

The Voice in Prayer

The *fourth* thing to be considered in the gift of prayer is the *voice*.

Though the beauty of our expressions and the tuneableness

of our voice can never render our worship more acceptable to God, the infinite Spirit, yet our natures, being composed of flesh and spirit, may be assisted in worship by the harmony of the voice of him that speaks. Should the matter, method, and expression be ever so well chosen in prayer, yet it is possible for the voice to spoil the pleasure and injure the devotion of our fellow-worshipers. When speeches of the best composure and warmest language are recited in a cold, harsh, or ungrateful way, the beauty of them is almost lost.

Some persons by nature have a very sweet and tuneful voice, that whatsoever they speak appears pleasing. Others must take much more pains and attend with diligence to rules and directions, that their voice may be formed to an agreeable pronunciation. For we find, by sad experience, that all the advantages that nature can obtain or apply to assist our devotions are all little enough to keep our hearts from wandering and to maintain delight. At least, it is a necessary duty to know and avoid those disagreeable ways of pronunciation that may rather disgust than edify such as join with us.

I confess, in secret prayer there is no necessity of a voice—for God hears a whisper, as well as a sigh and a groan. Yet some Christians cannot pray with any advantage to themselves without the use of a voice in some degree. Nor can I judge it at all improper, but rather preferable, so that you have a convenient place for secrecy. For hereby you will not only excite your own affections the more, but by practice in secret, if you take due care of your voice there, you may also learn to speak in public the better.

The great and general rule I would lay down for managing the voice in prayer is this: *Let us use the same voice with which we usually speak in grave and serious conversation, especially upon sensitive and affecting subjects.* This is the best direction that I know to regulate the sound as well as the words. Our own native and common voice appears most natural and may be managed with the greatest ease. And some persons have taken occasion to ridicule our worship and to censure us as hypocrites when we fondly seek and affect any new and different sort of sounds or voices in our prayers.

The particular directions for the use of the voice in prayer are such as these:

DIRECTION 1. *Let your words be all pronounced distinctly* and not made shorter by cutting off the last syllable; nor longer by the addition of hems and Oh's; of long breaths, affected groanings, and useless sounds; of coughing or spitting, etc. which some have heretofore been guilty of, and have sufficiently disgraced religion.

If you cut off and lose the last syllable of your word, or mumble the last words of the sentence and sink in your voice so that others cannot hear, they will be ready to think it is because you did not speak properly and so were afraid to be heard.

If on the other hand, you lengthen out your sentences with ridiculous sounds, you endanger the devotion even of the wisest and the best of your fellow-worshipers and expose the worship to the profane raillery of idle and corrupt fancies. While you seem to be designing to rub off the roughness of your throat, or to express greater affection by such methods, others will suspect that it is a method only to prolong your sentences, to stretch your prayers to an affected length, and to recover your thoughts what to say next. Therefore, when your passions happen to be elevated with some lively expression in prayer and you are delightfully constrained to dwell upon it, or when you meditate to speak the next sentence with propriety, it is far better to make a long pause and keep a decent silence than to fall into such indecencies of sound.

DIRECTION 2. *Let every sentence be spoken loud enough to be heard, yet none so loud as to affright or offend the ear.* Between these two extremes there is a great variety of degrees in sound sufficient to answer all the changes of our affections and the different sense of every part of our prayer. In the beginning of prayer especially, a lower voice is more becoming, both as it bespeaks humility and reverence, when we enter into the presence of God, and as it is also a great convenience to the organs of speech not to rise too high at first—for it is much harder to sink again afterwards than to rise to higher accents if need requires. Some persons have got a habit of beginning their prayers, and even upon the most common family occasions, so loud as to startle the company. Others begin so low in a large assembly that it looks like secret worship, and as though they forbid those that are present to join with them. Both these extremes are to be avoided with prudence and moderation.

DIRECTION 3. *Observe a due medium between excessive swiftness and slowness of speech; for both are faulty in their kind.*

If you are too swift, your words will be hurried on and will as it were intrude upon one another and be mingled in confusion. It is necessary, therefore, to observe a due distance between your words, and a much greater distance between your sentences, that so all may be pronounced distinctly and intelligibly.

Due and proper pauses and stops will give the hearer time to conceive and reflect on what you speak and more heartily to join with you, as well as give you leave to breathe and make the work more easy and pleasant to yourselves. Besides, when persons run on heedlessly with an incessant flow of words, being carried as it were in a violent stream, without rests or pauses, they are in danger of uttering things rashly before God, giving no time at all to their own meditation but indulging their tongues to run sometimes too fast for their own thoughts as well as for the affections of such as are present with them. And hence it comes to pass that some persons have begun a sentence in prayer and been forced to break off and begin anew. Or if they have pursued that sentence, it has been with so much inconsistency that it could hardly be reduced to sense or grammar—which has given too sensible an occasion to others to ridicule all conceived prayer, and has been very dishonorable to God and his worship. All this arises from a hurry of the tongue into the middle of a sentence, before the mind has conceived the full and complete sense of it.

On the other hand, if you are too slow, and very sensibly and remarkably so, this will also grow tiresome to the hearers, while they have done with the sentence you spoke last, and wait in pain and long for the next expression, to exercise their thoughts and carry on their devotion. This will make your worship appear heavy and dull. Yet I must needs say that an error on this hand in prayer is to be preferred before an excess of speed and hurry, and its consequences are less hurtful to religion.

In general, with regard to the two foregoing directions, *Let the sense of each sentence be a rule to guide your voice, whether it must be high or low, swift or leisurely*. In the invocation of God, in humble adoration, in confession of sin, in self-resignation, a slower and more modest voice is, for the most part, very becoming, as well as in every other part of prayer, where there is nothing very passionate expressed. But in petitions, pleadings, thanksgivings, and rejoicings in God, fervency and importunity, holy joy and triumph, will raise the voice some degrees higher, and lively passions of the delightful kind will naturally draw out our language with greater speed and spirit.

DIRECTION 4. *Let proper accents be put according as the sense requires*. It would be endless to give particular rules how to place our accents. Nature dictates this to every man, if he will but attend to the dictates of nature. Yet, in order to attain it in greater perfection and to secure us from irregularity in this point, let us avoid these few things following:

1. *Avoid a constant uniformity of voice,* that is, when every word and sentence are spoken without any difference of sound—like a boy at school, repeating all his lesson in one dull tone, which shows that he is not truly acquainted with the sense and value of the author. Now, though persons may be truly sincere and devout who speak without any difference of accent, yet such a pronunciation will appear to others as careless and negligent, as though the person that speaks were unconcerned about the great work in which he is engaged and as though he had none of his affections moved, whereby his voice might be modulated into agreeable changes.

2. *Avoid a vicious disposition of the accents, and false pronunciation.*

As for instance, it is a *vicious pronunciation* when a person uses just the same set of accents and repeats the same sets of sounds and cadences in every sentence, though his sentences are ever so different as to the sense, as to the length, or as to the warmth of expression—as if a man should begin every sentence in prayer with a high voice and end it in a low, or begin each line with a hoarse and deep bass and end it with a shrill and sharp sound. This is as if a musician should have but one sort of tune or one single set of notes, and repeat it over again in every line of a song, which should never be graceful.

Another *instance of false pronunciation* is when strong accents are put upon little words and particles which bear no great force in the sentence. And some persons are so unhappy that those little words *they* and *that,* and *of* and *by,* shall have the biggest force of the voice bestowed upon them, whilst the phrases and expressions of chief signification are spoken with a cold and low voice.

Another *instance of false pronunciation* is when a calm, plain sentence, wherein there is nothing emotional, is delivered with much force and violence of speech. Or when the most emotional and affectionate expressions are spoken with the utmost calmness and composure of voice. All which are very unnatural in themselves and to be avoided by those that would speak properly, to the edification of such as worship with them.

The *last instance* I shall mention of *false pronunciation* is when we fall into a musical turn of voice, as though we were singing instead of praying. Some devout souls have been betrayed into such a self-pleasing tone by the warmth of their spirits in secret worship—and having none to hear and to inform them how disagreeable it is to others, have indulged it even to an incurable habit.

3. *Avoid a fond and excessive humoring of every word and sentence to extremes, as if you were upon a stage in a theater*—which fault, also, some serious persons have fallen into for want of caution. And it hath appeared so like affectation that it hath given great ground for censure. As for instance:

If we should express every humble and mournful sentence in a weeping tone and with our voice personate a person that is actually crying—that is, what our adversaries have exposed by the name of *canting* and *whining*, and have thrown it upon a whole party for the same of the imprudence of a few.

Another instance of this excessive affectation is when we express every pleasurable sentence in our prayers, every promise of comfort, every joy or hope, in too free and airy a manner, with too bold an exultation or with a broad smile, which indeed looks like too familiar a dealing with the great

God. Every odd and unpleasing tone should be banished from divine worship. Nor should we appear before God in humility upon our knees, with grandeur and magnificence upon our tongues, lest the sound of our voice should contradict our gesture, lest it should savor of irreverence in so awful a presence and give disgust to those that hear us.

Gesture in Prayer

We proceed now to the fifth and last thing considerable in the gift of prayer, and that is, *gesture.*

And though it may not so properly be termed a part of the gift, yet inasmuch as it belongs to the outward performance of this piece of worship, I cannot think it improper to treat a little of it in this place.

Since we are commanded to pray always and at all seasons, there can be no posture of the body unfit of short ejaculations and pious yearnings towards God; while we lie in our beds, while we sit at our tables, or are taking our rest in any methods of refreshment, our souls may go out towards our heavenly Father and have sweet converse with him in short prayers. And to this we must refer that passage, 1 Chron. 17:16, concerning David, where it is said, "He sat before the Lord, and said, Lord, who am I, or what is my house, that thou hast brought me hitherto?" But when we draw near to God in special seasons of worship, the work of prayer calls for a greater solemnity, and in everything that relates to it we ought to compose ourselves to greater reverence, that we may worship God with our bodies as well as with our spirits, and pay him devotion with our whole natures. 1 Cor. 6:20.

In our discourse concerning the *gestures* fit for worship, we shall consider *first*, the posture of the whole *body*, and *sec-*

ondly, of the particular parts of it, and endeavor to secure you against indecencies in either of them.

1. Those *postures of the body*, which the light of nature and rule of Scripture seem to dictate as most proper for prayer, are *standing, kneeling*, or *prostration*.

Prostration is sometimes used in secret prayer, when a person is under a deep and uncommon sense of sin, and falls flat upon his face before God and pours out his soul before him, under the influence of such thoughts and the working of such graces as produce very uncommon expressions of humiliation and self-abasement. This we find in Scripture made use of upon many occasions, as, Abraham fell on his face before God, Gen. 17:3.; and Joshua before the Lord Jesus Christ, the Captain of the host of God, Josh. 5:14. So Moses, Ezekiel and Daniel, at other seasons. So in the New Testament, when John fell at the feet of the angel to worship him, supposing it had been our Lord. Rev. 19:10. And who could choose but fall down to the dust at the presence of God himself?

Kneeling is the most frequent posture used in this worship. And nature seems to dictate and lead us to it as an expression of humility or a sense of our needs—a supplication for mercy and adoration of, and a dependance upon, him before whom we kneel. This posture has been practiced in all ages and in all nations, even where the light of the Scripture never shone. And if it might be had with convenience, would certainly be a most agreeable posture for the worship of God in public assemblies as well as in private families, or in our secret chambers. There are so many instances and directions for this posture in Scripture that it would be useless to take pains to prove it. Song of Solomon, 2 Chron. 6:13; Ezra, Ezr. 9: 5, Daniel, Dan. 6:10; Christ himself, Luke 22:41; Paul, Acts 20:36 and 21:5, and Eph. 3:14.

In the last place, *standing* is a posture not unfit for this worship, especially in places where we have not conveniency for the humbler gestures. For as standing up before a person whom we respect and reverence is a token of that esteem and honor which we pay him, so standing before God, where we have not conveniencies of kneeling, is an agreeable testification of our high esteem of him whom we then address and worship. There are instances of this gesture in the word of God. Our Savior says to his disciples, "When ye stand praying" Mark 11:25; and "The publican stood afar off and prayed" Luke 18:13. Standing seems to have been the common gesture of worship, in a large and public assembly, 2 Chron. 20:4, 5, 13. And in this case it is very proper to conform to the usage of Christians with whom we worship, whether standing or kneeling, since neither of them is made absolutely necessary by the word of God.

But I cannot think that sitting or other postures of rest and laziness, ought to be indulged in solemn seasons of prayer, unless persons are in any respect infirm or aged, or the work of prayer be drawn out so long as to make it troublesome to human nature to maintain itself always in one posture. And in these cases, whatsoever gesture of body keeps the mind in the best composure and fits it most to proceed in this worship, will not only be accepted of God, but is most agreeable to him. For it is a great rule that he hath given, and he will always stand by, that bodily exercise profiteth little; for he looks chiefly after the heart, and he will have mercy and not sacrifice.

2. The *posture of the several parts of the body*, that are most agreeable to worship, and that may secure us from all indecencies, may be thus particularized and enumerated.

As for the head, let it be kept for the most part without motion, for there are very few turns of the head in the worship of prayer that can be accounted decent. And many persons have exposed themselves to ridicule by tossings and shakings of the head and nodding while they have been offering the solemn sacrifice of prayer to God. Though it must be allowed that in cases of great humiliation, the hanging down of the head is a proper method to express that temper of mind. So the praying publican, in the text afore-cited; so the Jews in the time of Ezra, in a full congregation bowed their heads and worshiped the Lord with their faces towards the ground. Neh. 8:6. But in our expressions of hope and joy it is natural to lift up the head while we believe that our redemption draws nigh, as in Luke 21:28. I might also mention the apostle's advice that "he that prays ought to have his head uncovered, lest he dishonor his head" 1 Cor. 11:4.

In the face, the God of nature hath written various indications of the temper of the mind, and especially when it is moved by any warm affection.

In divine worship the whole visage should be composed to gravity and solemnity, to express a holy awe and reverence of the majesty of God and the high importance of the work wherein we are engaged.

In confession of sin, while we express the sorrows of our soul, melancholy will appear in our countenances. The dejection of the mind may be read there, and according to the language of Scripture, shame and confusion will cover our faces. The humble sinner blushes before God at the remembrance of his guilt. Jer. 51:51, Ezra 9:6. Fervency of spirit in our petitions, and holy joy when we give thanks to our God for his mercies and rejoice in our highest hope, will be discovered by very agreeable and pleasing traces in the features and countenance.

But here let us take heed that we do not expose ourselves to the censure of our Savior, who reproved the Pharisees for disfiguring their faces all that day they set apart for secret fasting and prayer. Matt. 6:16. While we are engaged in the very duty, some decent appearances of the devotion of the mind in the countenance are very natural and proper, and are not here forbidden by our Lord. But at the same time, it is best that those discoveries or characters of the countenance should fall below and stay behind the inward affections of the mind, rather than rise too high, or than go before. The devotion of our hearts should be warmer and stronger than that of our faces. And we should beware of all irregular and disagreeable distortions of the face—all those affected grimaces and wringing of the countenance, as it were to squeeze out words, or our tears, which sometimes may tempt our fellow-worshipers to disgust when they behold us. As well as, on the other hand, avoid yawning, an air of listlessness, and drowsy gestures, which reveal the sloth of the mind. It is a terrible word spoken by Jeremiah, in another case, Jer. 48:10: "Cursed is he that doth the work of the Lord negligently."

To lift up the eyes to heaven is a very natural posture of prayer, and therefore the Psalmist so often mentions it, Ps. 121:1, and 123:1, and 96:8. Though sometimes, under great dejection of spirit and concern for sin, it is very decent, with the public, to look down, as it were, upon the ground, as being unworthy to lift up our eyes to heaven where God dwells. Luke 18:13.

But above all, *a roving eye*, that *takes notice of everything*, ought to be avoided in prayer. For though it may be possible for a person that prays to keep his thoughts composed whilst his eyes thus wander, (which at the same time seems very difficult,) yet spectators will be ready to judge that our hearts are given to wander as much as our eyes are, and they will suspect that the life and spirit of devotion are absent. Upon this account some persons have found it most agreeable to keep the eyes always closed in prayer, lest, by the objects that occur to their sight, the chain of their thoughts should be broken, or their hearts led away from God by their senses. Nor can I think it improper to shut that door of the senses, and exclude the world while we are conversing with God. But in this and other directions, I would always excuse such persons who lie under any natural weakness, and must use those methods that make the work of prayer most easy to them.

The *lifting up of the hands*, sometimes folded together or sometimes apart, is a very natural expression of our seeking help from God who dwells above, Ps. 28:2, and 134:2. The elevation of the eyes and the hands is so much the dictate of nature in all acts of worship wherein we address God that the heathens themselves frequently practiced it, as we have an account in their several writers, as well as we find it mentioned as the practice of the saints in the Holy Scriptures.

And as the elevation of the hands to heaven is a very natural gesture when a person prays for himself, so when a superior prays for a blessing to descend upon any person of an inferior character, it is very natural to lay his hand upon the head of the person for whom he prays. This we find practiced from the beginning of the world, and the practice descends throughout all ages. It is true indeed, this gesture, the imposition of hands, was used by the prophets and apostles when they pronounced authorative and divine blessings upon men and communicated miraculous gifts. But I esteem it not so much a peculiar rite belonging to the prophetical benediction as it is a natural expression of a desire of the divine blessing from a father to a son, from an elder person to one that is younger, from a minister to other Christians, especially those that are babes in Christ. And therefore, when a person is set apart and devoted to God in any solemn office, whilst prayers are made for divine blessing to descend upon him, imposition of hands seems to be a gesture of nature. And considered in itself, I cannot think it either unlawful or unnecessary.

With regard to the other parts of the body, there is little need of any directions. Calmness and quietness and an uniformity of posture seem to be more decent. Almost all motions are disagreeable, especially such as carry with them any sound or noise. For hereby the worship is rather disturbed than promoted, and some persons by such actions have seemed as though they beat time to the music of their own sentences.

In secret devotion indeed, sighs and groans and weeping may be very well allowed, where we give vent to our warmest passions and our whole nature and frame are moved with devout affections of the mind. But in public these things should be less indulged, unless in such extraordinary seasons when all the assembly may be effectually convinced they arise deep from the heart. If we indulge ourselves in various motions or noise made by the hands or feet or any other parts, it will tempt others to think that our minds are not very intensely engaged, or at least it will appear so familiar and irreverent as we would not willingly be guilty of in the presence of our superiors here on earth.

Family Prayer

Since it is so necessary for the person that speaks in prayer to abstain from noisy motions, I hope all that join with him will understand that it is very unseemly for them to disturb the worship with motion and noise. How indecent is it at family prayer for persons to spend a good part of the time in settling themselves upon their knees, adjusting their dress, moving their chairs, saluting those that pass by and come in after the worship is begun? How unbecoming is it to stir and rise while the two or three last sentences are spoken, as though devotion were so unpleasant and tedious a thing that they longed to have it over. How often is it found, that the knee is the only part that pays external reverence to God, while all the other parts of the body are composed of laziness, ease, and negligence! Some there are that seldom come in till the prayer is begun, and then there is a bustle and disturbance made for their accommodation. To prevent some of these irregularities, I would persuade him that prays not to begin till all that design to join in the family worship are present, and that even before the chapter is read. For I would not have the word of God used in a family for no other purpose than the tolling of a bell at church, to tell that the people are coming into prayers.

Grace Before and After a Meal

Since I have spoken so particularly about family prayer, I would insert a word or two concerning another part of social worship in a family, and that is, *giving thanks before and after a meal*. Herein we ought to have a due regard to the occasion and the persons present; the neglect of which hath been attended with indecencies and indiscretions.

Some have used themselves to mutter a few words with so low a voice as though by some secret charm they were to consecrate the food alone, and there was no need of the rest to join with them in the petitions. Others have broke out in so violent a sound as though they were bound to make a thousand people hear them.

Some perform this part of worship with a slight and familiar air, as though they had no sense of the great God to whom they speak. Others have put on an unnatural solemnity and changed their natural voice into so different and awkward a tone, not without some distortions of countenance, that hath tempted strangers to ridicule.

It is the custom of some to hurry over a single sentence or two, and they have done before half the company are prepared to lift up a thought to heaven. And some have been just heard to bespeak a blessing on the church and the king, but seem to have forgot they were asking God to bless their food, or giving thanks for the food they had received. Others again, have given themselves a loose into a long prayer, and among a multitude of other petitions have not had one that related to the table before them.

The general rules of prudence, together with a due observation of the custom of the place where we live, would correct all these disorders and teach us that a few sentences suited to the occasion, spoken with an audible and proper voice, are sufficient for this purpose, especially if any strangers are present. If we are *abroad in mixed company*, many times it is best for each person to lift up a petition to God in secret for himself. Yet, *in a religious family*, or where all the company are of a piece, and no other circumstance forbids it, I cannot disapprove of a pious soul sometimes breathing out a few more devout expressions than are just necessary to give thanks for the food we receive. Nor is it improper to join any other present occurrence of Providence together with the table worship.

Here I would also beg leave to add this, that when a person is eating alone, I do not see any necessity of *rising* always from his seat to recommend his food to the blessing of God, which may be done in any posture of body with a short ejaculation. Yet, when he *eats in company*, I am of opinion that the present custom of standing up is more decent and honorable than of sitting down just before we give thanks—which was too much practiced in the former age.

Thus I have delivered my sentiments concerning the *gestures proper for prayer*, and I hope they will appear useful and proper to maintain the dignity of the worship and to pay honor to God with our bodies as well as with our souls. As we mut not make ourselves mere statues and lifeless engines of prayer, so neither must we, out of pretense of spirituality, neglect all decencies. Our forms of religion are not numerous nor gaudy, as the Jewish rites, nor theatrical gestures, like the Papists. We have no need to be masters of ceremonies in order to worship God aright, if we will but attend to the simplicity of manners which nature dictates, and the precepts and examples that the gospel confirms.

Remark. Though the gestures that belong to *preaching* are very different from those of *prayer*, yet most of the rules that are prescribed for the expression and the voice in prayer may be usefully applied also to preaching. But this difference is to be observed, that in the work of preaching, the same restraints are not always necessary, and especially in applying truth warmly to the conscience. For then we speak to men in the name and authority of God, and we may indulge a greater freedom and brightness of language, more lively emotions, and bolder efforts of zeal and outward fervor. But in prayer, where in the name of sinful creatures we address the great and holy God, everything that belongs to us must be composed to an appearance of humility.

General Directions About the Gift of Prayer

Thus I have finished what I designed upon the Gift of Prayer, with regard to the *matter*, the *method*, the *expression*, the *voice*, and the *gesture*. I shall conclude this chapter with these *five general directions*.

I. *Keep the middle way between a nice and laborious attendance to all the rules I have given and a careless neglect of them*. As every rule seems to carry its own reason with it, so it is proper that there should be some regard had to it when occasions for the practice occur. For I have endeavored to say nothing on this subject but what might some way or other be useful towards the attainment of an agreeable gift of prayer and the decent exercise of that gift. The multiplicity of our wants, the unfaithfulness of our memories, the dullness and slowness of our apprehensions, the common wanderings of our thoughts, and the coldness of our affections, will require our best care for the remedy of them.

Yet, on the other hand, I would not have you confine yourselves too precisely to all these forms in matter, method, expression, voice and gesture, upon every occasion, lest you feel yourselves thereby under some restraint and prevent your souls of that divine liberty with which, upon special occasions, the Spirit of God blesses his own people in the performance of this duty. When the heart is full of good matter, the tongue will sometimes be "as the pen of a ready writer." Ps. 45:1. Such a fixedness and fullness of thought, such a fervor of pious affections, will sometimes produce so glorious a fluence and variety of pertinent and moving expressions, and all in so just a method, as makes it appear that the man is carried beyond himself and would be straitened and cramped by a careful attendance to rules.

See, then, that the graces of prayer are at work in your souls with power; let this be your first and highest care; and by a sweet influence this will lead you to a natural and easy performance of this duty according to most of the particular rules I have given, even without a nice and exact attendance to them. So, without attendance to the rules of art, a man may sometimes, in a very musical humor, strike out some inimitable graces and flourishes, and charm all that hear him.

II. Among ministers and among your fellow-Christians, *observe those that have the most edifying gifts.* And with regard to the matter, method, expression, voice, and gesture, endeavor to imitate them who are more universally approved of, and the exercise of whose talents is most abundantly blessed, to excite and maintain the devotion of all their fellow-worshipers. And at the same time also, take notice of all the irregularities and indecencies that any persons are guilty of in this worship, in order to avoid them when you pray.

III. *Use all proper means to obtain a manly presence of mind and holy courage in religious performances.* Though excess of bashfulness be a natural infirmity, yet if indulged in such affairs, it may become very culpable. There have been many useful gifts buried in silence through a sinful bashfulness in the person endowed with them. And generally all persons, when they first begin to pray in public, feel something of this weakness, for want of a due presence of mind—and it hath had different effects. Some person have lost that due calmness and temper which should govern their expressions, and have been driven on to the end of their prayer like a schoolboy hurrying his lesson over, or an alarm set a running, that could not stop till it was quite done. Others have hesitated at every sentence, and, it may be, felt a stop in their speech, that they could not utter any more. Others again, whose minds have been well prepared and furnished, have lost their own scheme of thoughts and made poor work at first, through mere bashfulness.

I grant that courage and a degree of assurance are natural talents, but they may also, in a great measure, be acquired by the use of proper means. I will here mention a few of them.

1. Get above the shame of being religious, that you may be dead to the reproaches of a wicked world and despise the jests and scandal that are cast upon strict godliness.

2. Make religious conversation your practice and delight. If you are but inured to speak to men concerning the things of

God without blushing, you will be enabled to speak to God in the presence of men with holy confidence.

3. Labor to attain this gift of prayer in a tolerable degree, and exercise it often in secret for some considerable time before you begin in public.

4. Take heed that your heart be always well prepared, and let the matter of your prayer be well premeditated when you make your first public attempts of it.

5. Strive to maintain upon your soul a much greater awe of the majesty of that God to whom you speak than of the opinions of those fellow-creatures with whom you worship— that so you may, as it were, forget you are in the company of men while you address the Most High God. Chide your heart into courage when you find it shy and sinking, and say, "Dare I speak to the great and dreadful God, and shall I be afraid of man?"

Now, in order to practice this advice well, the next shall be akin to it.

6. Be not too tender of your own reputation in these externals of religion. This softness of spirit, which we call *bashfulness*, has often a great deal of fondness for *self* mingled with it. When we are to speak in public, this enfeebles the mind, throws us into a hurry, and makes us perform much worse than we do in secret. When we are satisfied, therefore, that we are engaged in present duty to God, let us maintain a noble negligence of the censures of men and speak with the same courage as though none but God were present.

Yet, to administer farther relief under this weakness, I add,

7. Make your first attempts in the company of one or two, either of your inferiors, or your most intimate, most pious, and candid acquaintance, that you may be under no fear or concern about their sentiments of your performance. Or join yourself in society with some young Christians of equal stand-

ing and set apart times for praying together—which is an excellent way to obtain the gift of prayer.

8. Do not aim at length of prayer in your younger attempts, but rather be short, offer up a few more common and necessary requests at first, and proceed by degrees to enlarge and fulfil the several parts of this worship as farther occasion shall offer and as your gifts and courage increase.

9. Be not discouraged if your first experiments be not so successful as you desire. Many Christians have in time arrived at a glorious gift in prayer who, in their younger attempts, have been overwhelmed with bashfulness and confusion. Let not Satan prevail with you, therefore, to cast off this practice, and your hope, at once, by such a temptation as this.

10. Make it the matter of your earnest requests to God that you may be endowed with Christian courage, with holy liberty of speech and freedom of utterance; which the blessed apostle Paul often prays for. And you have every reason to hope that he who gives "every good and perfect gift" will not deny you that which is so necessary to the performance of your duty.

I proceed now to the fourth general direction.

IV. *Entreat the assistance of some kind Christian friend to give you notice of all the irregularities that yourselves may have been guilty of in prayers*, especially in your first years of the practice of this duty. And esteem those the most valuable of your friends who will put themselves to the trouble of giving you a modest and an obliging hint of any of your own imperfections. For it is not possible that we ourselves should judge of the tone of our own voice or the gestures that we ourselves may use, whether they be agreeable to our fellow-worshipers or not. And in other instances also, our friends may form a more unbiased judgment than ourselves; and therefore are fittest to be our correctors.

For lack of this, some persons in their youth have gained so ill a habit of speaking in public, and so many disorders have attended their exercise of the gift of prayer—ill tones, vicious accents, wild distortions of the countenance, and divers other improprieties, which they carried with them all the years of their life, and have oftentimes exposed the worship of God to contempt and hindered the edification of those that joined with them rather than promoted it.

V. *Be frequent in the practice of this duty of prayer, not only in secret, but with one another.* For though every rule that I have before given were fixed in your memories and always at hand, yet without frequent practice you will never attain to any great skill and readiness in this holy exercise.

As our graces themselves, by being often tried and put upon action, become stronger and shine brighter, give God more glory and do more service to men. So will it fare with every gift of the Holy Spirit also; it is improved by frequent exercise. Therefore the apostle bids the young evangelist Timothy that he should not neglect to stir up the gift that was in him, though it was a gift communicated in an extraordinary way by the imposition of hands, 2 Tim. 1:6. And therefore it is that some serious Christians that have less knowledge will excel persons of great learning and talents and judgment, in the gift of prayer—because, though they do not understand the rules so well, yet they practice abundantly more. And for the most part, if all other circumstances are equal, it will be found a general truth that he that prays most, prays best.

Facing Dry Seasons in Prayer

*"If we find our hearts, after all, very barren,
and hardly know how to frame a prayer
before God of ourselves, it has been oftentimes
useful to take a book in our hand, wherein are
contained some spiritual meditations in a
petitionary form, some devout reflections, or
excellent patterns of prayer. . . ."* (Page 55)

Who has tried praying for any extended time and has not run into this difficulty? It is a point at which it is easy to drop the habit, make excuses for skipping our times of secret prayer, and allowing busyness to crowd out this appointment with God. Surely this is one of the temptations of "the destruction that wastes at noonday" (Psalm 91).

We might well ask in such dry seasons to be shown what, if anything, is amiss in us that has caused the dry season to come. If there is any separation between us and God, we know that it has been caused by us rather than by him. The movement is on our part, not his. Once we have been shown, and have faced up to what is grieving the Holy Spirit, we can repent, make our confession, and be forgiven. Psalm 32 describes such a condition in dramatic graphicness. "When I declared not my sin, my body wasted away through my groaning all day long. For day and night thy hand was heavy upon me; my strength was dried up as by the heat of summer" (vv. 3 and 4).

We face here what may be a perennial problem for Christians: that our unrecognized sin is making a barrier between us and the Lord. I say "unrecognized" because our attitudes and inward sins not only may be hidden from others but from ourselves as well. Years ago, Gert Bohanna gave her testimony about being converted miraculously after three failed marriages and a suicide attempt. Her alcoholism was out of control, and she had no hope. Then God came into her life and delivered her into a new life. It is an amazing and moving story. But then she added, "I graduated from the gross sins in my past to Christian sins: self-righteousness, judgment, jealousy, resentment, unforgiveness, and self-pity."

Do we recognize that these inward attitudes matter to God? Do we realize that we do actually grieve the Holy Spirit by indulging in such hidden and inner sins? On the face of things we may look as though we are in good shape. But the dryness we feel, the distance from God, the lack of desire for fellowship with him may be pointers that we are indeed grieving the Holy Spirit. An unforgiving spirit toward another person who has wronged us may be a special problem, because we may feel justified in holding on to the desire to see that person judged.

It may be well in such a situation to spend some time in letting the searchlight of truth penetrate our souls. It could even be helpful if we have a mature friend or counselor who would truthfully tell us what they see that might be blocking our fellowship with God.

The use of books in fighting this spiritual malaise has its values and its perils. If we allow the books to act as a kind of "pump primer," to help us move from our lethargy to a more active frame of mind, they serve us well. Watts mentions especially using the psalms this way, certain passages from the prophets, and the epistles of Paul. We will find that the psalmists express their difficulties in praying in words more colorful than we would normally use.

"When my soul was embittered, when I was pricked in heart, I was stupid and ignorant, I was like a beast toward thee." (Psalm 73:21,22)

"Do not forsake me, O Lord! O my God, be not far from me! Make haste to help me, O Lord, my salvation!" (Psalm 38:21,22)

"My strength is dried up like a potsherd, and my tongue cleaves to my jaws; thou dost lay me in the dust of death." (Psalm 22:15)

But as we read any of the psalms, we are carried away from such preoccupation with our own state of mind and reminded that we are citizens of the Kingdom, children of the God of mercy. Over and over again we are reminded that God is sovereign and that he is working out his purpose in the events of life. What is said in the New Testament is even clearer in this regard, because it is all written in the light of the resurrection of our Lord Jesus Christ.

Again Watts comes to our aid with his hymns.

> Come, Holy Spirit, heavenly Dove,
>   With all thy quickening powers;
> Kindle a flame of sacred love
>   In these cold hearts of ours.
>
> In vain we tune our formal songs,
>   In vain we strive to rise;
> Hosannas languish on our tongues,
>   And our devotion dies.

> And shall we then forever live
>   At this poor dying rate?
> Our love so faint, so cold to thee,
>   And thine to us so great!
>
> Come, Holy Spirit, heavenly Dove,
>   With all thy quickening powers;
> Come, shed abroad the Savior's love,
>   And that shall kindle ours.

Or these stanzas from another hymn:

> Awake, our souls! Away, our fears!
>   Let every trembling thought be gone!
> Awake, and run the heavenly race,
>   And put a cheerful courage on!
>
> True, 'tis a strait and thorny road,
>   And mortal spirits *tire and faint*;
> But they forget the mighty God
>   That feeds the strength of every saint.
>
> From thee, the ever-flowing Spring
>   Our souls shall drink a fresh supply,
> While such as trust their native strength
>   Shall melt away, *and droop, and die.* (emphasis mine)

It has been the experience of believers all through the centuries that these dry times come in the spiritual life. One of the temptations that some people face is the desire to create the good feeling that we once have experienced. Could this be the reason that groups sometimes indulge in long periods of "uplifting" music—not so much to express the joy they feel in the Lord, but in the expectation that singing it will bring back the euphoric sensations they once enjoyed. It is true that singing, praising, lifting up the heart can help dispel spiritual depression, as I have mentioned earlier in this book. But there is a difference between genuinely giving oneself to praise because we want to offer it in spite of our feelings, and using it as a technique to make ourselves feel better.

Dry times sometimes simply have to be endured. We have to push past the deadness we feel into acts of obedience, having no particular expectation that we shall be repaid with an inrush of good, warm feeling, and trusting that the sacrifice of praise will be accepted.

Here is what one spiritual counselor has to say about feeling or lack of it in prayer:

> We do not realize that while a vivid consciousness of God, a flood of spiritual joy, the touch of inspiration, and the flame of fervor are all valid and desirable elements of prayer, they are not of its essence—they are certainly not its central object. Some of the most profound spiritual writers go so far as to confine them to the immature stages of prayer. They are the marks of the neophyte in Christ—the sugar-plums awaiting spiritual babes to tempt them to take the first step. While we need not concur in a judgment which is not borne out by Christian experience, we shall do well to recognize that vivid emotion in prayer is one of the most fruitful sources of self-deception and therefore one of its most formidable hindrances to true progress.
>
> For prayer, we must remember, is, first and foremost, an act of devotion; and devotion is not an affair of fervid feeling or tender sentiment, but a solemn act, whereby a man devotes, commits, consecrates himself wholly to God. Now, if such consecration means anything, it means a death of that self-will and self-love

which separate the soul from its true Source; and that type of prayer is surely best which most effectually mortifies our lower self. And no one who has had any experience of the spiritual life would care to maintain that prayer which is accompanied by a feeling of intense satisfaction and emotion is the most likely to purge us of self-love. On the contrary, the danger of such prayer is that it gives self-love a unique opportunity. Self feeds on emotional prayer, and gradually we forget that we are *in via*—on pilgrimage from self to God—and that we are making no progress unless prayer becomes increasingly a fight to the death between the self that battens upon emotional luxury and the love that claims that self as a living sacrifice. The central thing in prayer is not the garden of the soul, but the altar of dedication. If we can go to that altar with joy and singing, happy are we; but more blessed are those who ascend its steps in the nakedness of faith, giving all for all and asking nothing in return, save that the will of God may be fulfilled in them.[1]

[1] E. Herman, *Creative Prayer*: Paraclete Press, 1997, Chapter Four.

The Grace of Prayer

In the first two chapters I have finished what I proposed concerning the external parts of prayer. I proceed now to take a short view of the internal and spiritual part of that duty, and this has been usually called the grace of prayer. Here I should endeavor to explain what it means, and show how properly the term is used. Afterward I shall particularly mention what are those inward and spiritual exercises of the mind which are required in the duty of prayer, and then give directions how to attain them. But in the most part of this chapter I shall pass over things with much brevity, because it is not my design in writing this book to say over again what so many practical writers have said on these subjects.

What the Grace of Prayer is, and how it differs from the Gift

Grace, in its most general sense, implies the free and undeserved favor of one person towards another that is esteemed his inferior. And in the language of the New Testament, it is usually put to signify the favor and mercy of God towards sinful creatures—which, upon all accounts, is acknowledged to be free and undeserved. Now, because our natures are corrupt and averse to what is good, and whensoever they are changed and inclined to God and divine things, this is done by the power of God working in us. Therefore, this very change of nature, this renewed and divine frame of mind, is called, in the common language of Christians, by the name of Grace.

If I were to write my thoughts of the distinction between the terms, *virtue*, *holiness*, and *grace*, I should give them thus:

Virtue generally signifies the mere material part of that

which is good, without a particular reference to God as its principle or end. Therefore, the good dispositions and actions of the heathens were called virtues. And this word is also applied to sobriety, righteousness, charity, and everything that relates to ourselves and our neighbors, rather than to religion and things that relate to divine worship.

Holiness signifies all those good dispositions and actions, with their particular reference to God as their end, to whose glory they are devoted and performed. The word *holy* signifies that which is devoted or dedicated.

Grace denotes the same dispositions, with a peculiar regard to God as their principle, intimating that they proceed from his favor.

Sometimes this word is used in a comprehensive sense to signify the whole train of Christian virtues or the universal habit of holiness. So may those texts be understood, "And of his fullness have we all received, and grace for grace" John 1:16. "Grow in grace and in the knowledge of our Lord Jesus Christ" 2 Pet. 3:18. And so in our common language we say such a person is a graceless wretch; he has no *grace* at all, i.e., no good dispositions. We say such an one is truly gracious, or he has a principle of *grace*, i.e., he is a man of religion and virtue.

Sometimes it is used in a sense a little more enlarged, but not universal, and it implies all those pious qualifications that belong to any one action or duty. So we read of the grace that belongs to conversation—"Let your speech be always with grace" Col. 4:6. The *grace* of singing, "Singing with grace in your hearts"; and the *grace* of divine worship seems to be mentioned. "Let us have grace whereby we may serve God acceptably, with reverence," etc., Heb. 12:28, and the *grace* of prayer; "I will pour upon the house of David, the spirit of *grace* and supplications" Zech. 12:10.

The grace of prayer, in our common acceptation, is not any one single act or habit of the mind, but it implies *all those holy dispositions of soul which are to be exercised in that part of divine worship*. It consists in a readiness to put forth those several acts of the sanctified mind, will, and affections, which are suited to the duty of prayer.

Hence will appear the great difference that is betwixt the *gift* and *grace* of prayer. The *gift* is but the shape, the outer shell of the duty. The *grace* is the soul and spirit that gives it life and vigor and efficacy, that renders it acceptable to God and of real advantage to ourselves.

The *gift* chiefly consists in a readiness of thought agreeable to the several parts of prayer, and a facility of expressing those thoughts in speaking to God. The *grace* consists merely in the inward workings of the heart and conscience toward God and religion. The *gift* has a show and appearance of holy desires and affections, but holy affections, sincere desires, and real converse with God belong only to the *grace of prayer*.

The *gift* and the *grace* are many times separated one from the other. And it hath been often found that the gift of prayer hath been attained in a great degree by study and practice and by the common workings of the Spirit of God communicated to some persons that have known nothing of true grace. There may be also the *grace of prayer* in lively exercise in some souls who have but a very small degree of this gift, and that hardly know how to form their thoughts and desires into a regular method, or to express those desires in tolerable language.

Concerning some persons it may be said, as in Matt. 7:22, that though they could pour out abundance of words before God in prayer, though they could preach like apostles, or like angels, or cast out devils in the name of Christ, yet our Lord Jesus knows them not—for they have no grace. On the other hand, there are some that are dear to God, that can but chatter and cry like a swallow or a crane, as Hezekiah did, and yet are in the lively exercise of the grace of prayer. But where both these, the *gift* and the *grace*, meet together in one person, such a Christian brings honor to God and has a greater capacity and prospect of doing much service for souls in the world; he is made of great use to the edification and comfort of his fellow-Christians.

Those acts of the sanctified soul in all its powers which are put forth in the duty of prayer, may be properly called so many graces of the Holy Spirit drawn forth into exercise. And of these, *some belong to the whole work and worship* of prayer, and others are *peculiar to the several parts* of the duty.

General Graces of Prayer

The graces that belong to the whole work or duty of prayer are such as these:

1. *Faith, or belief in the being of God, and his perfect knowledge, and his gracious notice of all that we speak in prayer.* This rule the Apostle gives: "He that comes to God, must believe that he is, and that he is a rewarder of them that diligently seek him," Hebrews 9:6. We should endeavor to impress our minds frequently with a fresh and lively belief of God's existence, though he be so much unknown; of his presence, though he be invisible; of his just and merciful regard to all the actions of men, and especially their religious affairs; that so prayer may not be a matter of custom and ceremony, but performed with a design and hope of pleasing God and getting some good from him. This exercise of a lively faith runs through every part of the duty and gives spirit and power to the whole worship.

2. *Gravity, solemnity, and seriousness of spirit.* Let a light and trivial temper be utterly banished when we come into the

presence of God. When we speak to the great Creator (who must also be our Judge) about the concerns of infinite and everlasting moment, we ought to have our souls clothed with solemnity and not to assume those airs which are lawful at other seasons, when we talk with our fellow creatures about ordinary affairs. A wantonness and vanity of mind ought never to be indulged in the least degree, when we come to perform any part of divine worship, especially when we, who are but dust and ashes, speak unto the great and dreadful God.

3. *Spirituality and heavenly-mindedness* should run through the whole of this duty. For prayer is a retirement from earth and a retreat from our fellow creatures to attend on God and hold correspondence with him that dwells in heaven. If our thoughts are full of corn and wine and oil and the business of this life, we shall not seek so earnestly the favor and face of God, as becomes devout worshipers. The things of the world therefore must be commanded to stand by for a season and to abide at the foot of the mount, while we walk up higher to offer up our sacrifices, as Abraham did, and to meet our God. Our aims and ends and desires should grow more spiritual as we proceed in this duty. And though God indulges us to converse with him about many of our temporal affairs in prayer, yet let us take care that the things of our souls, and the eternal world, always possess the chief room in our hearts. And whatsoever of the cares of this life enter into our prayers and are spread before the Lord, let us see that our aims therein are spiritual, that our very desires of earthly comforts may be purified from all carnal ends and sanctified to some divine purposes, to the glory of God, to the honor of the gospel, and the salvation of souls.

4. *Sincerity and uprightness of heart* is another grace that must run through this worship. Whether we speak to God concerning his own glories, whether we give him thanks for his

abundant goodness, or confess our various iniquities before him, or express our desires of mercy at his hand, still let our hearts and our lips agree and not be found mockers of God who searches the heart, and tries the reins, and can spy hypocrisy in the darkest corners of the soul.

5. *Holy watchfulness, and intention of mind upon the duty* in which we are engaged must run through every part of prayer. Our thoughts must not be suffered to wander among the creatures and rove to the ends of the earth when we come to converse with the high and holy God. Without this holy watchfulness we shall be in danger of leaving God in the midst of the worship, because the temptations that arise from Satan and from our own hearts are various and strong. Without this watchfulness our worship will degenerate into formality, and we shall find coldness and indifference creeping upon our spirits, and spoiling the success of our duties. "Watch unto prayer" is a constant direction of the great Apostle. I might add to these, humility, and delight, or pleasure, and other exercises of the sanctified affections; but I shall have occasion more properly to mention them under the next heading.

Graces that Belong to Particular Parts of Prayer

These *graces* that peculiarly belong to the several parts of prayer are distinguished according to the parts of this duty, namely:

1. *Invocation*, or calling upon God, requires *a special awe of his majesty* to attend it and a *deep sense of our own lowliness and unworthiness.* And at the same time we should express holy wonder and pleasure that the Most High God, who inhabits eternity, will suffer such contemptible and worthless beings as we are to hold correspondence with him.

2. The work of *adoration*, or praise, runs through the several attributes of the divine nature and requires of us the exercise of our various affections suited to those several attributes. As when we mention God's self-sufficiency and independence, it becomes us to be humble and acknowledge our dependence. When we speak of his power and of his wisdom, we should abase ourselves before him because of our weakness and folly, as well as stand in holy admiration at the infinity of those glories of God. When we mention his love and compassion, our souls should return much love to him again, and have our affections going forth strongly towards him. When we speak of his justice, we should have an holy awe upon our spirits, and a religious fear suited to the presence of the just and dreadful God. And the thought of his forgiveness should awaken us to hope and joy.

3. In the *confession* of our sorrows and our sins, humility is a necessary grace, and deep contrition of soul in the presence of that God whose laws we have broken, whose gospel we have abused, whose majesty we have affronted, and whose vengeance we have deserved. Here all the springs of repentance should be set open, and we should mourn for sin, even at the same time we hope iniquity is forgiven and our souls are reconciled to God. Shame and self-indignation, and holy revenge against the corruption of our hearts, should be awakened in this part of prayer.

4. In our petitions we should raise our *desires to such different degrees of fervency* as the nature of our request makes necessary. When we pray for the things of the upper world and eternal blessings, we cannot be too warm in our desires. When we seek the mercies of life, the degree of fervency should be abated. For it is possible that we may be happy and yet go without many of the comforts of the present state. Submission is here required, and God expects to see his children thus rationally

religious, and wisely to divide the things which are most agreeable to his will and most necessary for our felicity.

5. While we make intercession for our friends or our enemies, we ought to feel in ourselves warm and lively compassion. And when we pray for the church of Christ in the world, we should animate all our expressions with a burning zeal for his glory and tenderness for our fellow-Christians.

Pleading with God calls for *humble importunity*. The arguments that we use with God in pleading with him are but the various forms of importunate request. But because we are but creatures, and we speak to God, humility ought to mingle with every one of our arguments. Our pleadings with him should be so expressed as always to carry in them that decency and that distance which becomes creatures in the presence of their Maker. In pleadings also we are required to exercise faith in the promises of the gospel, faith in the name of Christ Jesus our Mediator, faith in the mercies of our God, according to the discoveries he hath made of himself in his word. We are called to believe that he is a God hearing prayer, and that he will bestow upon us what we seek, so far as is necessary for his glory and our salvation: to believe that he is a rewarder of them who diligently seek him. Hebrews 11:6. Here also the grace of hope comes into exercise. For while we trust the promises, we hope for the things promised, or the things for which we petition. We ought to maintain an humble, holy expectation of those mercies for which we plead with God. We must direct our prayer to him, and look up with David, Ps. 5:3, and with Habakkuk, "stand upon our watch-tower and see what he will answer us," Hab. 2:1.

6. In that part of prayer which is called *profession* or *self-resignation*, great *humility* is again required; a sweet *submission to his will*; a composedness and quietness of spirit under his determination—even though for reasons of infinite wisdom

and love he withholds from us the particular comforts that we seek. Here let patience have its perfect exercise, and let the soul continue in an humble frame, waiting upon God. While we give up ourselves to God a divine steadiness of soul should attend it, and the *firmest courage of heart* against all oppositions, while we confirm all our self-dedications to the Lord.

7. In *thanksgiving* a most *hearty gratitude* of soul is required, a deep sense of divine favors, and a readiness to return unto God according to his goodness, to the uttermost of our capacities; a growing *love* to God, and *sincere longing to do something for him*, answerable to the variety and riches of his grace towards us. Here also with *holy wonder*, we acknowledge the condescension of God to bestow mercies upon us, so unworthy. And this wonder should arise and grow up in *divine joy*, while we bless our Maker for the mercies of this life and our Father for an interest in his covenant and his special love. And in our *thanksgivings* we should be sure to take notice of all returns of prayer, all merciful appearances of God in answer to our requests. For it is but a poor converse that is maintained with God if we are only careful about our speaking to him, but take no notice of any replies he condescends to make to our poor and worthless addresses.

8. When we *bless* God, we should show an *earnest longing after the honor of the name of God*, and our souls should breathe fervently after the accomplishments of those promises wherein he hath engaged to spread his own honors, and to magnify his name, and the name of his Son. We should, as it were, *exult* and *triumph* in those glories, which God, our God, possesses, and rejoice to think he shall forever possess them.

Then we *conclude* the whole prayer with our *amen of sincerity* and of *faith*, in one short word, expressing over again our adorations, our confessions, and our petitions; trusting and hoping for the hearing of our prayers and acceptance of our persons, from whence we should take encouragement to rise from this duty with a sweet serenity and composure of mind, and maintain a joyful and heavenly frame, as those that have been with God.

But lest some pious and humble souls should be discouraged when they find not these lively exercises of faith, hope, love, fervency of desire, and divine delight in worship, and thence conclude that they have not the *grace of prayer*, I would add this caution: That all the graces of prayer are seldom at work in the soul at once, in an eminent and sensible degree. Sometimes one prevails more, and sometimes another, in this feeble and imperfect state. And when a Christian comes before God with much deadness of heart, much overcome with carnal thoughts, and feels great reluctance even to the duty of prayer, and falls down before God, mourning, complaining, self-condemning, and, with sighs and deep groans in secret, makes known his burden and his sins to God; though he can but speak a few words before him, such a frame and temper of mind will be approved by that God who judges the secrets of the heart, and makes most compassionate allowances for the infirmity of our flesh; and will acknowledge his own grace working in that soul, though it be but just yearning and struggling upward through loads of sin and sorrow.

Directions to Attain the Grace of Prayer

In order to direct us in the spiritual performance of this duty, we must consider it as a holy converse maintained between earth and heaven, betwixt the great and holy God, and lowly and sinful creatures. Now the most natural rules that I can think of to carry on this converse are such as these:

DIRECTION 1. *Possess your hearts with a most affecting sense*

of the characters of the two parties that are to maintain this cor-
respondence; that is, *God and yourselves.* This, indeed, is one
direction for the gift of prayer, but it is also most necessary to
attain the grace. Let us consider who this glorious Being is that
invites us to this fellowship with himself: how awful in majesty!
how terrible in righteousness! how irresistible in power! how
unsearchable in wisdom! how all-sufficient in blessedness! how
condescending in mercy! Let us consider, who are we that are
invited to this correspondence? how vile in our original! how
guilty in our hearts and lives! how needy of every blessing! how
utterly incapable to help ourselves! and how miserable forever,
if we are without God!

And if we have sincerely obeyed the call of his gospel, and
have attained to some comfortable hope of his love, let us consider how infinite are our obligations to him, and how necessary, and how delightful it is to enjoy his visits here, with
whom it will be our happiness to dwell forever. When we feel
our spirits deeply impressed with such thoughts as these, we
are in the best frame and most likely way to pray with grace
in our hearts.

DIRECTION 2. When you come before God, *remember the*
nature of this correspondence: it is all-spiritual. *Remember the*
dignity and privilege, the design and the importance of it.

A sense of the high favor in being admitted to this privilege
and honor will fill your souls with humble wonder and with
heavenly joy, such as becomes the worshipers of an infinite
God. A due attendance to the design and importance of this
duty will fix your thoughts to the most immovable attention
and strict watchfulness. It will overspread your spirit with seriousness, it will command all your inward powers to devotion,
and will raise your desires to holy fervency. You pray to him
that hath power to save and to destroy, about your eternal
destruction, or eternal salvation. And if eternity, with all its

awful attendants, will not awaken some of the graces of prayer, the soul must be in a very stupid frame.

DIRECTION 3. *Seek earnestly a state of friendship with him with whom you converse, and labor after a good hope and assurance of that friendship.* "We are all by nature enemies to God, and children of his wrath" Rom. 8:7, and Eph. 2:2. If we are not reconciled, we can never hold communion with him. How can we delight in converse with an enemy so almighty or pay him due worship, while we believe he hates and will destroy us? But oh! how unspeakable is the pleasure in holding converse with so infinite, so almighty, and so compassionate a Friend! And how ready will all the powers of nature be to render every honor to him, while we feel and know ourselves to be his favorites, and the children of his grace! While we believe that all his honors are our glory in this state of friendship, and each of his perfections is a pillar of our hope, and an assurance of our happiness!

Now in order to obtain this friendship, and to promote this divine fellowship, I recommend you to the next direction.

DIRECTION 4. *Live much upon, and with, Jesus the Mediator, by whose interest alone you can come near God and be brought into his company.* "Christ is the way, the truth, and the life: and no man comes to the Father, but by him" John 14:6. "Through him Jews and Gentiles have access unto the Father" Ephesians 2:11. Live much upon him therefore by trust and dependence, and live much with him by meditation and love.

When a sinner under first conviction sees with horror the dreadful holiness of God, and his own guilt and deserving of damnation, how fearful is he to draw near to God in prayer! And how much discouraged while he abides without hope! But when he first beholds Christ in his mediatorial offices, and his glorious all-sufficiency to save, when he first beholds this new and living way of access to God, consecrated by the blood of Christ, how cheerfully doth he come before the throne of God and pour out his own soul in prayer! And how lively is his nature in the exercise of every grace suited to his duty! How deep his humility! How fervent his desire! How importunate his pleadings! How warm and hearty are his thanksgivings!

And we have need always to maintain upon our spirits a deep sense of the evil of sin, of our desert of death, of the dreadful holiness of God, and impossibility of our converse with him without a Mediator, that so the name of Jesus may be ever precious to us and that we may never venture into the presence of God in set and solemn prayer without the eye of our soul to Christ, our glorious Introducer.

DIRECTION 5. *Maintain always a praying frame*, a temper of mind ready to converse with God. This will be one way to keep all praying graces ever ready for exercise. Visit him, therefore, often and upon all occasions, with whom you would obtain some immediate communion at solemn seasons of devotion, and make the work of prayer your delight; nor rest satisfied till you find pleasure in it.

What advantages and opportunities soever you enjoy for social prayer, do not neglect praying in secret; at least once a day constrain the business of life, to give you leave to say something to God alone. When you join with others in prayer, where you are not the speaker, let your heart be kept intent and watchful to the work, that you may pray so much the better when you are the mouth of others to God.

Take frequent occasion, in the midst of your duties in the world, to lift up your heart to God. He is ready to hear a sudden sentence, and will answer the yearnings of a holy soul toward himself, in the short intervals and spaces between your daily affairs. Thus you may pray without ceasing, as the Apostle directs, and your graces may be ever lively. Whereas, if you only make your addresses to God in the morning and evening and forget him all the day, your hearts will grow indifferent in worship and you will only pay a salutation with your lips and your knees, and fulfill the task with dull formality.

DIRECTION 6. *Seek earnestly the assistance of the Holy Spirit.* It is he that works every grace in us, and fits us for every duty. It is he that awakens sleeping graces into exercise. It is he that draws the soul near to God and teaches us this correspondence with heaven. He is the spirit of grace and supplication; but because this is the subject of the following chapter, I shall pursue it no farther here.

Keeping a Praying Frame

*"Maintain always a praying frame, a temper
of mind ready to converse with God. This will
be one way to keep all praying graces ever
ready for exercise. Visit Him, therefore, often
and upon all occasions, with whom you would
obtain some immediate communion at solemn
seasons of devotion, and make the work of
prayer your delight; nor rest satisfied till you
find pleasure in it."* (Page 127)

It should be no surprise to us that we have difficulty experiencing a "spirit of prayer" in church or in our quiet times if we go through most of the rest of the day heedless of God and his presence in us. We would treat no friend or loved one like that—moving through the day in their presence and ignoring them all the while. Yet this is, for all practical purposes, what many of us do: we "say our prayers" and then go about our business. We even may feel a little rushed in saying our prayers, because other things are competing for our attention, and we can hardly wait to get through our little "shopping list" of requests.

In my first experience as a pastor, I called on a young man to pray, I think, at choir rehearsal. Since my own walk with the Lord was relatively new and still fresh, I assumed the same for others. To my great embarrassment and that of my friend, he fumbled for words, and his prayer didn't make sense at all. After that, I was more cautious about whom to ask to pray aloud in a group.

Another person I knew used to carry around a table grace with her, because she was afraid that she would be asked to say grace at women's meetings, and she did not trust herself to be able to get out the right words at the time. Yet in both cases, the person who was asked to pray had no trouble in simply talking with others. It was the idea of praying that brought fear and self-consciousness to the surface.

What can we do to make prayer more natural, more like our best conversation with other persons? Watts says, "Maintain always a praying frame." We can move through our days with our minds fully occupied with our responsibilities, and yet keep that praying frame of mind. It is a matter of inner conversation with the Lord while we carry on other duties. There is no way that one can so concentrate on a single subject that no other thoughts come into the mind. Even if our labor is mental, requiring intense concentration, we are still aware of other things. Just so, we can from time to time renew our conversation with God. It may be nothing more than "Jesus, have mercy on me." Or it may be, "Thank you, Father, for giving me this challenge." Or it may even be reduced to saying, "Jesus!" or, "Thank you," or, "Help, Lord." My mother used to say, when any trouble came up, "Lord, have mercy!"

We have to decide whether we are going to be independent souls, making our own way, charting our own course, and leaning on our own understanding—or whether we are going to be dependent on God, knowing that his wisdom is greater than our own, that he knows the way we should go and has a will for us, and that he gives grace to those who ask it. It is not a matter of going to him in the morning and receiving a stock of grace for the day. It is a matter of relationship, of a continual connection between our spirits and the Holy Spirit. Maintaining a praying frame is just that—"maintaining."

What are some of the things that interfere with keeping this frame of mind? The first thought that comes to me is *sin, disobedience*. If we are in conscious violation of what we know to be right and good, this will certainly preclude and obstruct the spirit of prayer. We cannot violate and grieve the Holy Spirit and expect that he will keep a loving glow of his presence in our hearts.

There are some sins that lurk within the heart without calling much attention to themselves, and certainly without crying out that they are blocking the praying frame of mind. I think of such things as deeply held resentments toward a person or persons. Situations may have occurred in our lives that caused hurt and pain. If we have not let God deal with these in his love and mercy, if we have not sought a forgiving spirit toward those who hurt us, and if we are holding on to our "right" to be resentful and bitter toward that person or persons, then the praying frame of mind will be strangely absent from us. Jesus said it as clearly as possible when he said that before going to the altar we must be reconciled with our brother. Is it not possible that our prayers and the fruit of our prayers are greatly impaired by the resentments we harbor, some of which we do not even consciously remember? If we are interested in cultivating a praying frame of mind, we will need to do some "housecleaning."

Of course the old sin of pride is ever ready to squelch the desire to lean on God. The Pharisee in Jesus' parable (Luke 18:9-14) prayed only so that he could boast about his spiritual achievements. "God, I thank you I am not like other men. . . ." That kind of prayer is not only odious in the eye of God, it is contemptible in the ears of others, and that's why Jesus used it as he did. If we try to disguise our pride and appear humble, we may fool ourselves, and we may even fool others for a time. But it will not deceive God, and the true praying frame of heart and mind will flee from us.

One of the ways of keeping a praying frame of mind is to recall the love by which God has drawn us to himself. Who can express the debt we owe Watts for the immortal words of the hymn, "When I survey the wondrous cross"?

> When I survey the wondrous cross
>   On which the Prince of glory died,
> My richest gain I count but loss,
>   And pour contempt on all my pride.
>
> Forbid it, Lord, that I should boast,
>   Save in the death of Christ, my God;
> All the vain things that charm me most—
>   I sacrifice them to his blood.
>
> See from his head, his hands, his feet
>   Sorrow and love flow mingled down.
> Did e'er such love and sorrow meet,
>   Or thorns compose so rich a crown?
>
> Were the whole realm of nature mine,
>   That were a present far too small.
> Love so amazing, so divine,
>   Demands my soul, my life, my all.

The same sentiments are expressed in another of his hymns, also sung by millions for generations.

> Alas! and did my Savior bleed?
>   And did my Sovereign die?
> Would he devote his sacred head
>   For such a worm as I?

Was it for crimes that I have done
   He groaned upon the tree?
Amazing pity! Grace unknown!
   A love beyond degree!

Well might the sun in darkness hide,
   And shut his glories in,
When Christ, the mighty Maker, died
   For man the creature's sin.

Thus might I hide my blushing face
   While his dear cross appears;
Dissolve my heart in thankfulness,
   And melt my eyes in tears.

But drops of grief can ne'er repay
   The debt of love I owe;
Here, Lord, I give myself away—
   Tis all that I can do.

Such hymns not only make appropriate themes to be sung in congregational worship, but also are useful for one's private prayer times, to help us vividly remember the Savior whom we love.

Do we regard prayer as a duty or as a delight? Is it optional or obligatory? Here again, we might compare it with a relationship we have with a loved one. Do we consider conversation with that person a duty or a delight? Is it optional or obligatory? Or are those questions irrelevant to the relationship when it is alive and important to us? We would hardly think of it in those terms at all—for the relationship would naturally produce an ongoing communication, heart to heart, spirit to spirit.

That is what God intends for us in relation to him.

The Spirit of Prayer

*A*ll the rules and directions that have hitherto been laid down in order to teach us to pray will be ineffectual if we have no divine aids. We are not sufficient of ourselves to think on thought, and all that is good comes from God. If, therefore, we would attain the gift or grace of prayer, we must seek both from heaven. And since the mercies of God of this kind, that are bestowed on men, are usually attributed to the Holy Spirit, he may very properly be called the Spirit of prayer. And as such, his assistance is to be sought with diligence and importunity.

I confess the spirit of prayer, in our language, may sometimes signify a temper of mind well furnished and ready for the work of prayer. So when we say, there was a greater spirit of prayer found in churches in former days than now, we mean there was a greater degree of the gift and grace of prayer found amongst men, their hearts and their tongues were better furnished and fitted for this duty. But to deny the spirit of prayer in all other senses, and declare there is no need of any influences from the Holy Spirit to assist us to pray, carries in it a high degree of self-sufficiency and borders upon profaneness.

My business, therefore, in this chapter shall be to prove by plain and easy arguments that the Spirit of God doth assist his people in prayer; then to show what his assistances are and how far they extend, that we may not expect more from him than Scripture promises, nor attribute too little to his influences; and after a few cautions laid down, I shall proceed to give some directions how the aids of the Holy Spirit may be obtained.

Proofs of the Assistance of the Spirit of God in Prayer

The methods of proof which I shall use to demonstrate the influences of the Spirit of God in prayer, are these three:

(1) Express texts of Scripture.

(2) Collateral texts.

(3) The experience of Christians.

I. The *first argument* is drawn from such express texts of Scripture as these:

1ST TEXT. Zech. 12:10. "I will pour out on the house of David and the inhabitants of Jerusalem, a Spirit of grace and of supplications." Here the Holy Spirit of God is called a Spirit of supplications, with respect to the special operations and ends for which he is here promised. The plentiful communications of his operations to men is often expressed by pouring him out upon them, as Isa. 44:3, Prov. 1:23, Tit. 3:6, and many other places. Now, that this prophecy refers to the times of the gospel is evident, because the effect of it is a looking to Christ as pierced or crucified. "They shall look on him whom they have pierced."

OBJECTION. Some will say, this promise only refers to the Jews at the time of their conversion.

ANSWER. Most of these exceeding great and precious promises that relate to gospel times, are made expressly to Jacob and Israel, and Jerusalem and Sion, in the language of the Old Testament. And how dreadfully should we deprive ourselves, and all the Gentile believers, of all these gracious promises at one stroke, by such a confined exposition! Whereas the apostle Paul sometimes takes occasion to quote a promise of the Old Testament made to the Jews, and applies it to the Gentiles; as 2 Cor. 6:16, 17, 18, "I will dwell with them and walk among them, and I will be their God, and they shall be my people," which is written for the Jews; in Lev. 26:12, "Come out from among them touch no unclean thing and I will be a father to you," etc. which are recited from Isa. 52:11 and Jer. 31:1, 9, where Israel alone is mentioned. And yet, in 2 Cor. 7:1 the apostle says "Having therefore these promises, dearly beloved, let us cleanse ourselves." Etc. And thus he makes the Corinthians, as it were, possessors of these very promises. He gives also much encouragement to do the same when he tells us, Rom. 15:4, "Whatsoever things were written afore time, were written for our learning, that we, through patience, and comfort of the Scriptures, might have hope." And ver. 8, 9, he assures us, that Jesus Christ confirms the promises made to the fathers, that the Gentiles may glorify God for his mercy. Again, in 2 Cor. 1:20, "All the promises of God in him are yea and in him amen, to the glory of God." Now it would have been to very little purpose to have told the Romans or the Corinthians of the stability of all the promises of God, if their faith might not have embraced them.

We are said to be blessed with faithful Abraham, if we are imitators of his faith, Gal. 3:29. If we are Christ's, then are we Abraham's seed, and heirs according to the promise; heirs by faith of the same blessings that are promised to Abraham, and to his seed, Rom. 4:13. Now this very promise, the promise of the Spirit, is received by us Gentiles, as heirs of Abraham, Gal. 3:14. That the blessings of Abraham might come on the Gentiles through Jesus Christ, that we might receive the promise of the Spirit through faith.

Being interested, therefore, in this covenant, we have a right to the same promises, so far as they contain grace in them, that they may be properly communicated to us. And therefore the house of David, in this prophecy of Zechariah, doth not only signify the natural descendants of David the king, but very properly includes the family of Christ, the true

David—believers that are his children, and inhabitants of Jerusalem, and members of the true church, whether they were originally Jews or Gentiles. For in Christ Jesus men are not known by these distinctions; there is neither Jew nor Greek. Gal. 3:28.

2ND TEXT. Luke 11:13. After Christ had answered the request of his disciples, and taught them how to pray, by giving them a pattern of prayer, he recommends them to ask his father for the Holy Spirit, in order to a fuller and farther assistance and instruction in this work of prayer, as the whole context seems to intimate.

3RD TEXT. Rom. 8:26. "The Spirit helpeth our infirmities, for we know not what to pray for as we ought; but the Spirit itself maketh intercession for us with groanings, which cannot be uttered." This cannot be interpreted as though the Holy Spirit assumed the work of Christ, who is our proper Intercessor and Advocate. For the Spirit, not being clothed with human nature, cannot properly be represented under such an inferior character as the nature of prayer or petition seems to imply. Whereas our Lord Jesus Christ, being man as well as God, may properly assume the character of a Petitioner. The business of the Holy Spirit therefore, is, to teach and help us to plead with God in prayer for the things which we want. And this will appear evidently by the next Scripture.

4TH TEXT. Gal. 4:6. "God hath sent the Spirit of his Son into our hearts, crying, 'Abba, Father.'" That is, the Spirit of God inclines and teaches us to address God in prayer as our Father. And so it is explained, Rom. 8:15. "Ye have received the spirit of adoption, whereby we cry, 'Abba, Father.'" It may be noted here, that this spirit of adoption belongs to every true Christian, in more or less degrees, otherwise the apostle's reasoning would not appear strong and convincing. "Because ye are sons, he hath sent forth the Spirit of his Son," Etc.

5TH TEXT. Eph. 6. "Praying always with all prayer and supplication in the Spirit, and watching thereunto with all perseverance." These words, EN PNEYMATI (*in the Spirit*), have reference to the work of the Spirit of God in us; for so the word EN PNEYMATI signifies in other places in the New Testament, Matt. 12:21. "I cast out Devils by the Spirit of God" Luke 2:27. "He came by the Spirit into the temple" 1 Cor. 12: 8, 9. "To one is given by the Spirit, the word of wisdom; to another knowledge, by the same Spirit," Etc. In this verse of the Epistle to the Ephesians, it cannot properly signify praying with our own spirit; that is, with the intention of our own minds, because that seems to be implied in the next words, watching thereunto.

OBJECTION. Some will say still, that this praying in the spirit was to be performed by an extraordinary gift, which was communicated to the apostles, and many others in the first age of Christianity. Something like the gift of tongues at Pentecost, and various gifts among the Corinthians, when they prayed, and preached, and sung by inspiration. See 1 Cor. 14.

ANSWER. Whensoever there was of extraordinary and miraculous communications of the Spirit in those first days of the gospel, we pretend not to the same now. But the assistances of the Spirit whereof we speak are, in some measure, attainable by Christians in all ages. For in this, Eph. 6:18, praying in the Spirit is enjoined on all believers, and at all times, with all sorts of prayer. Now it is not to be supposed that at all times and in all sorts of prayer, Christians should have this extraordinary gift.

We may also further remark, that the gift of prayer itself is not expressed as such an extraordinary and miraculous gift. Neither in the prophecy of Joel, chap. 2, nor in Acts, chap. 2, where that prophecy of Joel is accomplished. Nor is it mentioned particularly in the epistles of St. Paul among the miraculous gifts of the Holy Spirit in those places where they are enumerated. But only the gift of prayer in an unknown tongue seems to be spoken of in 1 Cor. 14, which rather refers to the gift of tongues than to that of prayer. And it is not unlikely that the omission or silence of the gift of prayer in those texts might be designed for this very purpose: that though there were gifts of prayer by immediate inspiration in those days, yet that there should be no bar laid against the expectation of Christians, in all ages, of some divine assistance in prayer, by a pretense that this was only an extraordinary gift to the apostle and the first Christians.

6TH TEXT. James 5:16, which we translate, "the effectual fervent prayers of the righteous." In the original it is DEESIS ENERLOEMENE, the inwrought prayer. The word is used to signify persons possessed of a good or evil spirit, and it signifies here prayer wrought in us by the good spirit that possesses us, that leads us and guides us. And the word is used in this sense several times in 1 Cor. 11, where the gifts of the Holy Spirit are spoken of. Yet let it be observed that here the apostle is speaking of such an inwrought prayer as all Christians might be capable of, for his epistle is directed to all the scattered tribes of Israel, Jam. 1:1, and he bids them all confess their faults to one another, that they might be healed—and for this reason, because the inwrought prayer of the righteous availeth much.

The last text I shall mention is Jude, ver. 20. "Praying in the Holy Ghost, keep yourselves in the love of God." Now this Epistle is written to all that are sanctified by God the Father, preserved and called in Jesus Christ, ver. 1. They are all directed to pray by the assistance of the Holy Ghost. And those who have not this spirit, in ver. 19, are said to be sensual.

I confess, the Holy Spirit hath been in a great measure so long departed from his churches, that we are tempted to think that all his operations in exhortations, in prayer and preaching, belong only to the first age of Christianity, and the extra-ordinary ministers, prophets and apostles. And it was from this absence of the Spirit that men proceeded to invent various methods to supply the want of him in prayer, by pater nosters, beads, litanies, responses, and other forms, some good and some bad, to which they confined the churches, to keep up the form of worship and the attention of the people, and at best, are left by many teachers to the use of our mere natural pow-ers, our reason, and memory. Hence spring those reproachful expressions about the spirit of prayer and the endless labor of men to make this word signify only the temper and disposition of the mind. So the spirit of adoption, in their sense, is noth-ing but a child-like temper, and the spirit of prayer means nothing else but a praying frame of heart.

But since some texts expressly speak of the Holy Spirit as working these things in us, since in many Scriptures the Spirit of God is promised to be given us, to dwell in us, and to be in us, and to assist in prayer, why should we industriously exclude him from the hearts of the saints, and thrust him out of those Scriptures wherever the words will possibly endure any other sense?

It is, in my opinion, much more natural and reasonable for us to interpret those places where the Spirit is mentioned, according to the plain language of clear texts, where the name of God's own Spirit is written.

However, if a man will but allow the Spirit of God, and his assistances in prayer to be mentioned in any one text of Scripture, so far as to be persuaded and encouraged thereby to seek those assistances that he may pray better, I will not be angry with him, though he cannot find this Spirit in every text, where others believe he is spoken of and designed.

II. The *second argument* for the aids of the Holy Spirit in prayer, is drawn from collateral Scriptures; and such are all those texts which represent the blessed Spirit as the spring of all that is good in us and show us that all other duties of the Christian life are to be performed in and by this Holy Spirit. Saints are born of this Spirit, John 3:6. Are led by the Spirit, Rom. 8:14. Walk in the Spirit, Gal. 5:16. Live in the Spirit, verse 25. By this Spirit mortifying the deeds of the body, Rom. 8:13. The Spirit convinces of sin, John 16:9, and fits us for confession. The Spirit witnesseth with our spirit, that we are the children of God, Rom. 8:16, and thereby furnishes us with thanksgivings. The Spirit sanctifies us and fills us with love and faith, and humility. And every grace that is needful in the work of prayer. Why then should men take so much pains to hinder us from praying by the spirit, when it is only by the Spirit we can walk with God, and have access to God? Eph. 2:18.

III. The *third argument*, to prove that the Spirit of God doth sometimes assist men in the work of prayer, is the experience of all Christians with regard to the grace of prayer, and many Christians in the exercise of the gift. The great difference that is between some believers and others in this respect, even where their natural abilities are equal; and the difference that is between believers themselves, at different times and seasons, seems to denote the presence or absence of the Holy Spirit. Some persons at some special seasons, will break out into a divine rapture in prayer, and be carried far beyond themselves. Their thoughts, their desires, their language, and everything that belongs to their prayer, seem to have something of heaven in them.

I will allow that in some persons this may ascribed to a greater degree of understanding, invention, fancy, memory, and natural affections of the mind, and volubility of the tongue. But many times also it shall be observed that those persons who have this gift of prayer in exercise do not excel nor equal the rest of their neighbors in fancy, invention, passion or eloquence. It may be they are persons of very crude parts, and below the common capacity of mankind.

Nor can it be always imputed to an overflow of animal nature, and warm imagination at those times when they are carried out in prayer thus beyond themselves. For this happens sometimes when they find their natural spirits not raised nor exalted. But the powers of nature labor perhaps under a decay and great languishing. And they can hardly speak or think about common affairs. I wish these testimonies to the aids of the Holy Spirit were more frequent among us.

REFLECTION. And it may be remarked that those who despise this gift of the Holy Spirit will deride the persons that pretend to any share of it, as foolish, stupid and ignorant; and will represent them generally as unlearned and sottish, dull and unthinking. And yet when this objection is made, whence comes this fluency, this fervor and this wonderful ability of pouring out the soul before God in prayer, which the scoffers themselves cannot imitate? Oh, then it is attributed to our wit, our memory, our invention, our fancy, our vehement affections, our confidence or impudence—to any thing rather than to the Spirit of God, because they are resolved to oppose his power, and deny his work in the hearts of believers.

I might here add citations from the article and liturgy of the church of England to confirm the doctrine of the aids of the Holy Spirit in our religious performances. "We have no power to do good works, pleasant and acceptable to God without the grace of God by Christ preventing of that we may have good will, and working with us when we have that good will," Art. 10. "The working of the spirit drawing up the mind to high and heavenly things," Art. 17. "And this ordinary work of the Holy Spirit in all believers is called the inspiration of the Holy Spirit," Art 13. "O God, from whom all holy desires, all good counsels, and all just works do proceed," Second Collect at evening prayer. And a little after: "Almighty God, who hast given us grace to make our common supplications." And in the Collect, the fifth Sunday after Easter, "Grant that, by thy inspiration, we may think those things that be good, and, by thy merciful guiding, may perform the same." Again, "Almighty God, of whose only gift it cometh that thy faithful people do unto thee true and laudable service," 13th Sunday after Trinity. "Grant that thy Holy Spirit may in all things direct and rule our hearts," 19th Sunday after Trinity. Homily 16th p. 1, 2, asserts the secret and mighty working of God's Holy Spirit which is within us; for it is the Holy Ghost and no other thing, stirring up good and godly motions in their hearts. Many more expressions of this kind might be collected from the homilies and public prayers of the church of England, so that one would think none of that communion should throw reproach and scandal upon the assistances of the Holy Spirit in good works and religious duties.

How Far the Spirit Assists Us in Prayer.

It is evident, then, that there is such a thing as the assistance of the Spirit of God in the work of prayer. But how far this assistance extends is a farther subject of inquiry, and it is very necessary to have a just notion of the nature and bounds of this divine influence, that we may not expect more than God has promised nor sit down negligently contented, without such degrees as may be attained.

Persons in this, as in most other cases, are very ready to run away with extremes. They either attribute too much or too little to the Holy Spirit.

In my judgment, those persons attribute too little to the Spirit of Prayer:

1. Who say there is no more assistance to be expected in prayer, than in any ordinary and common affair of life—as when the ploughman breaks the clods of his ground and casts in the wheat and the barley, his God doth instruct him to discretion, and teach him. Isa. 78:24, 25, 26. But this is, in effect, to deny his special influences.

2. Those who allow the Spirit of God merely to excite some holy motions in the heart while they pray, and to awaken something of grace into exercise, according to the words of a prayer. But that he does nothing towards our obtaining the ability or gift of praying, nor at all assists us in the exercise of the gift with proper matter, method or expression.

I persuade myself, the Scriptures cited in the foregoing section, concerning praying in the Spirit, can never be explained this way, in their full meaning; and I hope to make it apparent in this section that the Holy Spirit hath more hand in prayer than both these opinions allow.

I think, also, on the other hand, those persons expect too much from the Spirit in our day:

1. *Who wait for all their inclinations to pray, from immediate and present dictates of the Spirit of God*, who will never pray but when the Spirit moves them. I find in Scripture frequent exhortations to pray and commands to pray always, i.e., to pray upon all occasions. Yet I find no promise nor encouragement to expect the Holy Spirit will, by sudden and immediate impulses in a sensible way, dictate to me every season of prayer. For though the Spirit of God should sometimes withdraw himself in his influences, yet my duty and obligation to constant prayer still remain.

2. *Those who expect such aids of the Holy Spirit as to make their prayers become the proper work of inspiration;*

such as the prayers of David and Moses, and others recorded in Scripture. Let us not be so fond as to persuade ourselves that these workings of the Holy Spirit in ministers or in common Christians, while they teach, or exhort, or pray, arise to the character of those miraculous gifts that were given to the apostles and primitive believers—such as are described in the church of Corinth, and elsewhere. For at those times, a whole sermon, or a whole prayer together, was a constant impulse of the Holy Spirit, perhaps for the words as well as all the matter of it, which made it truly divine. But in our prayers, the Spirit of God leaves us a great deal to ourselves, to mingle many weaknesses and defects with our duties, in the matter, and in the manner, and in the words; so that we cannot say of one whole sentence that it is the perfect or the pure work of the Spirit of God. And we should run the danger of blasphemy, to entitle the Spirit of God to everything that we speak in prayer, as well as to exclude all his assistance from all the prayers of the saints in our day.

3. *Those who hope for such influence of the Spirit as to render their own study and labors needless*; who never have given diligence to furnish themselves in a rational way with an ability to pray, upon presumption of those divine impulses; nor upon any occasion will premeditate beforehand, but rush upon the duty, as Peter went out at Christ's command to walk upon the water, and hope to be upheld and carried through all the duty without their own forethought. They will cite the text which was given to the disciples, "When they deliver you up, take no thought how or what ye shall speak; for it shall be given you in that same hour what you shall speak," Matt. 10:19. But this text has quite another design.

It may be questioned whether this word of Christ forbids them all premeditation, but only an anxious and solicitous fear and care, as we are bid to take no thought for the morrow,

Matt. 6:34; i.e., be not over solicitous or disquieted about pro-
vision for the morrow. But if Christ did utterly forbid them all
preparation, yet that command and promise to the apostles in
miraculous times, when they should appear before magis-
trates, can never be given to encourage the sloth and laziness
of every common Christian in our day, when he appears in
worship before God.

Now, in order to find the happy medium between these
two extremes, of attributing too much or too little to the Spirit
of prayer, I have diligently consulted the word of God. And so
far as I am able to judge or determine, his assistance in prayer
may be reduced to the following particulars.

I. *He bestows upon us our natural capacities*, some degree
of understanding, judgment, memory, invention, and natural
affections, some measure of confidence, and liberty of speech,
and readiness to utter the conceptions of our mind.

And this he doth to believers in common with other men;
for every good gift comes from God, James 1:17. And in a particular manner, the third person in the Trinity, the Holy Ghost,
is generally represented as the Agent in such operations, especially where they relate to religion.

II. *He blesses our diligence in reading, hearing, meditation,
study and attempts at prayer*; whereby, while we attend to useful rules and instructions, we treasure up a store of matter for
this duty and learn by degrees to express our thoughts with
propriety and decency, to our own and other's edification.

Thus he adds a blessing to our studies, in order to grow in
the knowledge of the things of God as Christians; and in the
learning of tongues to interpret Scripture; and in the holy skill
of exhortation, in order to become able ministers.

As these are called spiritual gifts, because (as is before
shown) in the primitive times, they were given on the sudden,

in an extraordinary manner, without laborious study to acquire them. But in our day, these are to be obtained and improved by labor and use, by repeated trials, by time and experience, and the ordinary blessings of the Spirit of God— and the same must be said concerning the Gift of prayer. He sanctifies memory to treasure up such parts of the Holy Scriptures as are proper to be used in prayer; he makes it faithful to retain them, and ready in the recollection of them at proper seasons.

If men become skillful in any faculty, and especially in that which belongs to religion, it is justly attributed to God and his Spirit; for if he teaches the ploughman to manage wisely in sowing and reaping, Is. 28:26, 29, much more doth he teach the Christian to pray. He divides to everyone what gifts he pleases, and works according to his good pleasure, 1 Cor 12 from ver. 4 to ver. 11. All secondary helps and means, when well attended to and well applied, are made successful by his powerful benediction. And we may say to those Christians who have the greatest gifts in prayer, "Who made thee to differ from another? And what hast thou that thou hast not received?" 1 Cor. 4:7. For if we live not by bread alone, but by every word of power and blessing that proceeds from the mouth of God, Matt. 4:4, much more may we say concerning the spiritual improvements of the mind, that they are not attained by our labor alone but by the good Spirit of God making our labor prosperous.

III. *He inclines our hearts to pray and keeps them intent upon the work.* By nature there is in men an estrangedness from God: and there is too much of it remaining in the best. There is a natural reluctance to the duties of immediate communion with God, and a weariness in them. It is only the Spirit of God that works a heavenly frame in us, that makes us ready to pray always, and excites us to take occasion from the several concerns of our souls, or from the affairs of life, to go to the mercy-seat, and to abide there. It is he that kindly and secretly suggests, "now is the accepted time." The Spirit says to the soul secretly, "seek my face"; and the soul replies, "thy face, O God, will I seek," Ps. 27:8. And the spirit saith, come to God by prayer, as well as to Christ by faith, Rev. 22:19.

It is he that enlarges the desires towards God, and gives silent intimations of audience and acceptance. By his good motions he overcomes our delay and answers the carnal objections of our sinful and slothful hearts. He gives our spirits liberty for the work, as well as in it, and recalls our thoughts from wandering from God in worship, whether they be drawn away by our eyes, or our ears, or our busy fancies, or the suggestions of the evil one. It is the Holy Spirit that holds us to the duty in opposition to all discouragements, and makes us wrestle and strive with God in prayer, pour out our hearts before him, and stir up ourselves to take hold of him, agreeable to the language of those Scriptures, Gen. 32:24, Rom. 15:30, Ps. 72:8, Isa. 54:7. Now the means which the Spirit of God generally uses to bring us to prayer, and keep us to the duty, is by working in our souls a lively sense of the necessity and advantage of it, or giving us some refreshment and delight in and by it.

And if, when we are engaged in our worldly affairs, or in divine worship, the devil is permitted by sudden violent impressions on the fancy, to draw our hearts away to sinful objects, why should it be counted a strange thing that the blessed Spirit should cast in holy motions and encouragements to the duty?

IV. *He oftentimes, by his secret teachings, supplies us with the matter of prayer.* This is the express language of Holy Scripture, Rom. 8:26. "The Spirit helpeth our infirmities; for we know not what to pray for as we ought, but the Spirit itself maketh intercession for us," and that, according to the mind or will of God, ver. 27. All the senses that the wit of man has contrived to put upon this Scripture, to exclude the work of the Spirit of God, are very much forced and strained, to make them signify any thing else.

It is plain that we "know not what is good" for ourselves, Eccles. 6:12, and we of ourselves should often ask for things hurtful to us, James 4:3. We are not acquainted with our own needs, nor the method of our relief. It is the Spirit that must convince us of sin and righteousness; of our sin, and the righteousness of Christ, John 16:9. He is a Spirit of illumination in all the affairs of religion. It is he alone that searches the deep things of God, that knows what God hath prepared for believers, 1 Cor. 2:9. And therefore he makes intercession, or teaches us to pray for things agreeably to the divine will and purpose. He now and then also gives a hint of some argument to plead with God, either the name or mediation of Christ, or some of his own promises in the gospel, for he is promised to take of the things of Christ and show them unto us, John 16:26, and John 16:13, 14, 15. It is he that brings divine things to our remembrance—such things as are suited to the several parts of prayer. He sets the glory and the majesty of God before our eyes, and furnishes us with matter of adoration. By bringing sin to our remembrance, he fits us for confession, and by causing us to reflect on our many mercies, richly supplies us with thanksgivings.

Now, since the evil spirit is said to pluck the good seed of the word of God out of the heart, Matt. 12:19, why may we not suppose the good spirit to put good thoughts into the heart, to prepare and furnish us for such a duty as prayer? And such kind of influences as these, are called the good motions of the Spirit of God; which Christians of almost every sect and persuasion will allow, in some degree.

V. *When the Spirit of God supplies in us largely with matter in prayer, he doth in some measure influence the method too.* Method is but the disposition of the materials of a prayer, one after another. Now, as it is not possible our tongues should speak all these together, so it is not possible our mind should receive all the kind hints of them from the Spirit at once, but successively one after another, as seems good to him. Sometimes he fills our souls with so deep and penitent a sense of our past sin that we break out before God into humble confessions in the very beginning of prayer: "O Lord, I am vile, what shall I answer thee? Mine iniquities are gone over my head, and the number of them is infinite." And perhaps the soul dwells upon its humiliations through almost all the time of worship.

At another time the Spirit works as the Spirit of joy and thanksgiving, and the first words the lips utter are the language of gratitude and praise: "I thank thee, Father, Lord of heaven and earth that, though the mysteries of the gospel are hidden from the wise and prudent, yet thou hast revealed them unto babes."

Sometimes the soul is so inflamed with desire after such a particular grace or mortification of some special sin, that almost from every part of prayer, from adoration, confession, thanksgiving, etc., it will fetch some argument for bestowing that mercy, and at every turn insert that special petition, enforcing it with new arguments and pleadings.

Thus, though the beautiful connection of one sentence with another, and the smooth and easy transition from one part of prayer to another, be left much to ourselves, yet the mere order of those materials which the Holy Spirit gives in while we pray will be in some degree under his direction or influence. And if we may understand those words of Elihu, in a literal sense, Job 37:19, we have need of assistance in matter, method, and everything, when we speak to God. And we may well cry out, "Lord teach us what we should say to thee; for we cannot order our speech by reason of darkness": we need light and instruction from thee to frame our speeches, and to put them in order.

VI. *The Spirit may be said to give some assistance also toward apt and proper expression in prayer.* For he concurs in an ordinary way to the exercise of our natural and acquired faculties of knowledge, memory, vivacity of spirit, readiness of speech, and holy confidence whereby we express those thoughts which he hath excited in us in a becoming manner. And this he doth also in preaching and conferring upon the things of God, and this more eminently in the work of prayer, so that hereby a believer is able at all times to pour out his soul before God with a fullness of thought and variety of expression, to the great comfort of his own soul and the edification of his fellow-worshipers. St. Paul speaks of this boldness and utterance as a spiritual gift, 1 Cor. 1:5, and 2 Cor. 8:7. And he often prayed for this confidence and freedom of speech, this PARRESIA in preaching, Eph. 6:19; Col. 4:3, 4. And we also have reason to ask it of God in prayer; for it is as necessary also in that duty for carrying on the work of grace in our hearts, and the building up of the church, the body of Christ for which all gifts are given.

I might add also that as the Holy Spirit frequently, by secret hints, supplies us with the matter of prayer, he by that very means assists us toward expression; for expression is but the clothing of our thoughts or ideas in proper words. Now, in this state where the soul and body are so united, most of the ideas and conceptions of our mind are so joined to words that words arise, as it were, mingled with those ideas or conceptions which the Holy Spirit awakens within us. And we may humbly hope that when he hath given us some secret whispers what we should pray for, he will at least so far enable us to use proper expressions as may convey the same thoughts and matter to those who join with us in worship.

Especially when proper materials of prayer are brought to our mind in Scripture expressions, in some sense these are words "which the Holy Ghost teacheth"; that Spirit which is promised to bring to our remembrance the things which Christ hath taught us. But this is more evidently so at that time, when, together with these expressions, the graces of prayer are wrought up to a lively exercise, which is the next step of the assistance of the Spirit.

VII. *He excites in us those graces which are suited to the duty of prayer.* He spiritualizes our natural affections and fixes them on proper objects, and enlarges and heightens their activity. When sin is recollected, he awakens anger, shame and sorrow. When God is revealed to the mind in glory and justice, he overspreads the soul with holy awe and humble fear. When the Lord Jesus Christ and his redemption are upon the thoughts, the Holy Spirit warms and raises our desire and love. We are in ourselves cold and dead to spiritual things; he makes us lively in prayer and holds us to the work. He begets a holy reverence of God while we adore him. He works in us delight in God, and longing desires after him; fervency and importunity in our petitions for spiritual mercies; submission and resignation to the will of God in temporal things; faith in our Lord Jesus Christ, and hope in the promises of the gospel, while we plead with God for an answer to our prayers. He fills us also with holy joy and exultation in God, while we recollect in prayer his glories or his benefits, and awakens all the springs of thankfulness.

As these qualities in their first operation are attributed to the Spirit of God, (which is not my present business to prove,) so in their constant exercise in every duty, they want his farther assistance and efficacy, since of ourselves an apostle could say, "we are not sufficient for one good thought," 1 Cor. 3:5, but all our sufficiency is of God. It is God of his good pleasure, worketh in us both to will and to do, Phil. 2:13. He gave us sincere aims and designs in our petitions; for as to the manner of our prayers, there is the assistance of the Spirit necessary, as well as to the matter; and it is hinted in the text before cited. Rom. 8:26—We know not what to pray for as we ought, but the Spirit helpeth us. He influences our minds with a true and upright aim at the glories of God and our salvation; for otherwise we are ready to ask good things amiss, that we may spend them on our lusts.—James 4:3.

This work of the Spirit in awakening our graces, (though it be mentioned last,) yet it often begins before the prayer, and precedes his other influences, or our own labor in speaking to God.

Thus have I delivered my sentiments at large concerning the extent of the influences of the Spirit of God in prayer, and have shown how he qualifies us habitually for prayer, actually disposes and prepares us for it, and gives us present assistance in it. And after all, I would say that the most considerable and common assistance in prayer, which is peculiarly attributed to the blessed Spirit, as a Spirit of prayer, and may be expected from him in our day, consists chiefly in this: the putting our souls into a praying frame, the stirring up holy motions and yearnings after God, giving secret hints of our real wants, and of arguments and promises to plead with God, awakening the graces of love, fear, hope and joy, that are suited to this duty— and it is chiefly upon this account that he is called a Spirit of grace and supplication. When these are raised to a high degree, the heart will have a natural influence upon the invention, the memory, the language, and the voice. Out of the abundance of the heart the mouth will speak. And, for the most part, the utterance will be proportionable to the degree of inward affection and to the natural and acquired abilities of the person that prays; excepting some rare and glorious instances, where men are carried beyond themselves, by the uncommon presence of the Divine Spirit.

I might venture upon this subject to make an address to those persons who will entertain nothing in religion but what appears agreeable to principles of reason and philosophy, and yet have taken liberty to scoff at divine assistances in the duty of prayer. Let me entreat you, sirs, to tell me what there is in this doctrine that is unreasonable to assert or unbecoming a philosopher to believe? If the great God has required every man to pray, and will hear and reward the humble and sincere worshiper, why may we not suppose he is so compassionate as to help us in this work which he requires? Is he not full of goodness, and ready to accept those sinners that return to him? And why shall not the same goodness incline him to assist those that desire and attempt a return! Why may he not by secret impressions draw farther the desires of the soul that already breathes after him, when he sees the Spirit willing and feeble; and thus sweetly encourage the worship he delights in, and prepare his servants for his own reward?

This address may be repeated to Christians that profess the doctrine of the Holy Trinity, with much more force and argument. Do you believe the Almighty God sent his own Son to teach us how to pray? And when we are taught the right way, why may not his own spirit assist in the performance? Hath Jesus Christ purchased heaven for us, and may not the Spirit be permitted to incline us to ask for that heaven, and awaken our desires to seek it? When the Son of God saw us perishing in guilt and misery, did he descend, and relieve and save us, by dying for us? And when the Spirit of God beholds a poor creature willing to receive this relief and salvation, and yet is afraid to venture into the presence of an offended God, why may he not give secret hints of encouragement, and draw out the addresses of the heart and lips to a God that is willing to pardon? When he sees an humble sinner laboring and striving to break through temptations, to lay aside vain thoughts, to put carnal things far away from the mind, and to converse with God alone, why may he not impress some divine thoughts upon him, stir up devout and strong affections, make him surmount his difficulties, and raise him a little towards his heavenly Father? Since he has given him faculties of memory, intention and speech, why may he not assist those faculties when directed toward himself, and make them swifter and warmer in their advances towards God? To what purpose is the blessed Spirit mentioned so often in the New Testament as one that helps forward the salvation of men? To what purpose does he sustain so many characters and offices of Scripture? And to what end is he so often promised to Christians, to be with them, and to dwell in them, as a most glorious blessing of the gospel, if he be not permitted to do so much as this in assisting men to draw near to their Maker, and helping the children of God on earth to converse with their Father who is in heaven? Now, if such condescensions as these are not unworthy of the blessed God, why should it be unworthy of man or a Christian to believe them, and hope for them!

Cautions About the Influences of the Spirit

There are many practical cases that arise upon this subject of the assistance of the Spirit of prayer, which exercise the thoughts of honest and pious persons. It is not my purpose here to enlarge in this way. Yet that I may prevent or obviate some difficulties, I would lay down these few cautions:

I. FIRST CAUTION. *Do not believe all manner of impulses or urgent impressions of the mind to go and pray; proceed always from the blessed Spirit.*

Sometimes the mere terrors of conscience, awakened under a sense of guilt and danger, urge a natural man to go to prayer. So the sailors in Jonah's ship, when surprised with a storm, each of them fell a praying. Though the Spirit of God in his own operations makes much use of the consciences of men to carry on his own work, yet when these inward impulses to pray arise, merely from some affrighting providence or sudden conviction and torment of mind, and thus drag us into the presence of God, without any assistance to perform the duty, and without much regard to the success of the duty, we may justly fear the Holy Spirit of God hath not much hand in such impulses; for he both assists in the duty, and makes us solicitous about the success of it.

Sometimes Satan may so far transform himself into an angel of light as to hurry and impel a person to go and pray. But his impulses are generally violent and unreasonable. When we are engaged in some other business that is the proper duty of that season, he tyrannically commands, in a moment, to leave all and go aside and pray. But the Spirit of God draws us to God at a fit season, so as never to thrust out another necessary duty toward God or toward men. He is a God of order, and his Spirit always excites to the proper duty of the hour. Wherefore Satan would but divert us from one business by forcing us away to another, and then leave us to our own weakness in it and vex us afterwards with accusations.

II. SECOND CAUTION. *Do not expect the influences of the Spirit of prayer should be so vehement and sensible as certainly to distinguish them from the motions of your own spirits*: for the Spirit of God generally acts towards his people agreeably to the dispensation under which they are, either in a more sensible or a more imperceptible way.

Under the Old Testament the Spirit of God often carried the prophets away, as if it were in an ecstasy beyond themselves. Their style, their gesture, as well as inward commotions of heart, were frequently different from the common manner of men, and did sufficiently evidence to themselves, and in some measure to others also, that they were under the impressions of the Holy Spirit at special seasons.

Under the New Testament, the apostles had a more constant and habitual assistance of the Spirit, though it was extraordinary also, and in a calmer way were influenced in prayer and preaching more agreeable to rational nature: though, without doubt, they themselves well knew when they were under the certain conduct of the Holy Spirit.

In our day, when we have no reason to expect extraordinary inspirations, the Spirit of God usually leads us in so soft and silent a manner, agreeable to the temper of our spirits and concurrent circumstances of life, that his workings are not to be easily distinguished by ourselves or others, from the rational motions of our own hearts, influenced by moral arguments; though by the whole tendency, and the sanctifying effects, we know we had some assistance of the blessed Spirit.

Such are his operations generally in conversion, sanctification and consolation. He works so continually and sweetly with our own spirits, that we cannot certainly distinguish his working by any vehemence or strength of impression; but it is best known by the savor and relish of divine things that we then feel in our souls, and by consequent fruits of satisfaction in our hearts and lives.

III. THIRD CAUTION. *Though we have not any sure ground to expect extraordinary influences from the Spirit of prayer in our day, yet we ought not to deny them utterly*, for God hath nowhere bound himself not to bestow them. The chief ends for which immediate inspirations were given are long ceased among us where the gospel is so well established. Yet there have not been lacking instances in every age, of some extraordinary testimonies of the Spirit of God to the truth of the gospel, both for the conviction of unbelievers and for the instruction, encouragement, and consolation of his own people.

In the *conversion of a sinner*, the Spirit's work is usually gradual, and begun and carried on by providences, sermons, occasional thoughts, and moral arguments, from time to time, till at last the man is become a new creature and resolves heartily to give himself up to Christ, according to the encouragement of the gospel. Yet there are now and then some surprising and sudden conversions, wrought by the overpowering influences of the Holy Spirit, something like the conversion of St. Paul.

In the *consolation of saints*, the Spirit generally assists our own minds in comparing their hearts with the rule of the word, and makes it appear, they are the children of God, by finding the characters of adoption in themselves; this is his ordinary way of witnessing. But there are instances when the Spirit of God hath in a more immediate manner spoken consolation, and constrained the poor trembling believer to receive it; and this hath been evidenced to be divine, by the humility and advancing holiness that hath followed it.

So it is in prayer. The ordinary assistances of the Spirit, given in our day to ministers, or private Christians, in their utmost extent, imply no more than what I have described in the foregoing chapter. But there are instances where the Spirit of God hath carried a devout person in worship far beyond his own natural and acquired powers, in the exercise of the gift of prayer, and raised him to all uncommon and exalted degree of the exercise of praying graces, very near to those divine impulses which the primitive Christians enjoyed.

If a minister in a public assembly has been enabled to make his addresses to God with such a flow of divine eloquence, and spread the cases of the whole assembly before the Lord in such expressive language that almost everyone present hath been ready to confess, "Surely he knew all my heart"; if they have all felt something of a divine power attending his words, drawing their hearts near to the throne, and giving them a taste of heaven; if sinners have been converted in numbers, and saints have been made triumphant in grace, and received blessed advances towards glory: I would not be afraid to say "Surely, God is in this place," present with the extraordinary power and influence of his Spirit.

If a Christian hath been taught by this Spirit making intercession in him to plead with God for some particular mercy in such an unwonted strain of humble and heavenly argument, that he has found in himself secret and inward assurances that the mercy should be bestowed by something of a prophetical impulse, and has never been mistaken; if grace has been in vigorous exercise in the prayer, and afterward the success has always answered his expectation, I should not forbear to believe the extraordinary presence of the Spirit of prayer with him at that season. Dr. Winter, in Ireland, and several ministers and private Christians of the last age in Scotland, are notable and glorious instances of this gracious appearance of the Holy Spirit.

If a serious and humble worshiper, that hath long been seeking after the knowledge of some divine truth, should find himself enlightened upon his knees with a beam of heavenly light shining upon that truth with most peculiar evidence, and teaching him more in one prayer than he had learned by months of labor and study, I should venture to acknowledge the immediate aids and answer of the Spirit of prayer and illumination. Luther is said to have enjoyed such divine favors at the reformation of the church.

If a holy soul hath been conflicting with doubts and fears, and waiting upon God in all its appointed ways of grace, seeking consolation and assurance of the love of God; if while he hath been at the throne of grace, he has beheld God as his God, smiling and reconciled, and, as it were, seen the work of God on his own heart, in a bright and convincing light, and perhaps, by some comfortable word of Scripture impressed on his thoughts, hath been assured of his love to God, and the love of God to him; if from that immediate sensation of divine love he has been filled with joy unspeakable, and full of glory, as well as warmed with heavenly zeal for the honor of God, his God and Father: I must believe such a one to be sealed as a child of God, by the sweet influences of the Spirit of adoption, teaching him to pray, and cry, Abba, Father.

But concerning such workings of the Spirit of God as these are, because there have been many vain and foolish pretenses to them, I would make three remarks.

1. These are rare instances, and bestowed by the Spirit of God in so sovereign and arbitrary a manner, according to the secret counsels of his own wisdom, that no particular Christian hath any sure ground to expect them. Though I am persuaded there are many more instances of them in secret, among pious and humble souls, than ever came to public notice.

2. They are best judged of and distinguished from the mere effects of a warm fancy and from the spirit of delusion, not so much by the brightness and vehemence of the present impression as by their agreeableness to the standing rule of the word of God, and their influence towards humility and growing holiness. There is, therefore, the same rule to judge of the uncommon as well as the common assistances of this Spirit of supplication.

3. How near soever these rare and extraordinary impulses come to the inspiration of the apostles and first Christians in

the truth and power of them, yet they fall far short in the distinct evidence; for the Spirit of God hath not taught us so far to distinguish any particular parts or paragraph, even of such an extraordinary prayer, as that any one can say. These are perfect inspirations—because he would have nothing stand in competition with his written word, as the rule of faith and practice of his saints.

IV. FOURTH CAUTION. *Do not make the gift of prayer the measure of your judgment concerning the spirit of prayer.* If we follow this rule, there are three cases where we maybe led into mistake.

The first case is *when the gift is in great and lively exercise.* Beware of believing all those persons pray by the Spirit who pronounce very pious expressions with great seeming fervency and much volubility of speech, when it may be that their behavior and character in the world is sinful and abominable in the sight of God. It is true, indeed, the Spirit of God sometimes bestows considerable gifts upon persons that are unconverted; but we are not immediately to believe that everything that is bright and beautiful is the peculiar work of the Spirit in our day, unless we have some reason to hope the person is also one of the sons of God.

Much less can we suppose that noisy gesture, a distorted countenance, violence, and vociferation, are any signs of the presence of the Divine Spirit. Sometimes, indeed, the extraordinary anguish of mind, or inward fervor of affection, have extorted from the Saints of God loud complaints and groanings. David sometimes practiced this, as appears in his Psalms. Jesus Christ himself, when pressed with sorrows heavier than man could bear, offered strong cries and tears in the days of his flesh, Heb. 5:7, and we are sure the Spirit of prayer was with him. But there may be great noise, and violent commotions used to make a show of fervency and power, and with a design to make up the lack of inward devotion. God himself was indeed present at Sinai with thunder and lightning, and the sound of a trumpet once, Exodus 19. But another time, when he came down to visit Elijah, he was not in the earthquake, nor in the tempest, but in the still small voice, 1 Kings 19.

I would not impute the difference betwixt the prayers of one minister and another, one Christian and another, merely to the presence or absence of the Holy Spirit. Natural constitutions, capacities, acquirements, natural affections, and providential circumstances, can make a great difference. Nor would I impute the difference that is betwixt the prayers of the same true Christians, at different seasons only, to the unequal assistances of the blessed Spirit. For many other things may occur to make them more or less cold or fervent, dull or lively, in the exercise of the gift of prayer.

The *second case* wherein we may be in danger of mistake is where there is but a small measure of the gift of prayer. How ready are some persons to judge the Spirit of prayer is absent from the heart of that person that speaks to God if he hath but a crude and contemptible gift! If he seems to repeat the same things over again; if he labors under want of words, or expresses his thoughts in improper or disagreeable language; if he hath no beauty of connexion betwixt his sentences, and hath little order or method in the several parts of prayer. Now, though such persons that have so very small and despicable a talent should not be forward to speak in prayer in a great assembly, or among strangers, till by practice, in a more private way, they have attained more of this holy skill; yet there may be much of the Spirit of prayer in the hearts of some such persons as these.

It may be, they are young Christians lately converted, and are but beginning to learn to pray. The business of praying is a new work to them, though their zeal be warm and their hearts lively in grace. And natural bashfulness may sometimes hinder the exercise of a good gift of prayer.

Or it may be, they have very low natural parts—a poor invention, and memory, a barrenness of words, or some difficulty, or unhappiness in their common way of expressing themselves about other affairs. They may be some of those foolish things of this world, that God hath called to the knowledge of his Son, and filled their hearts with rich grace; but grace doth not so far exalt nature as to change a dull genius, and low capacity into a sprightliness of thought, and vivacity of language.

Or perhaps they have long disused themselves from praying in public; and at first, when they are called to it again, they may be much at a loss as to the gift of prayer, though grace may be in its advances in the soul.

Or perhaps they are in the lively exercise of deep humility and mourning before God, under a sense of guilt, or overwhelmed with fears of divine desertion, or conflicting and wrestling hard with some hurrying temptation, or under a present depression of mind, by some heavy sorrow; and may be in the case of David, when he was so troubled that he could not speak, Psalm 77:4.

Or, finally, God may withhold from them the exercise of the gift of prayer, to punish them with shame and confusion for some neglected duty, and chastise them, it may be, for carelessness in seeking after this holy skill of speaking to God, though some grace, such as zeal and love, may be at work in the heart.

Sometimes it may happen that the Spirit of prayer is communicated in a great degree to an humble Christian, who falls into many thoughtless indecencies of gesture in prayer, or delivers his sentences with a most unhappy tone of voice. Perhaps he was never taught to practice decency when he was young, and such ill habits are not easily cured afterwards. We are not, therefore, to despise and be offended at all such prayers, but endeavor to separate what is pious and divine from the human frailty and weakness, to pity such persons heartily, and be so much the more excited ourselves to seek after everything that is agreeable in the gift of prayer.

The *third case*, wherein we are in danger of mistake, is, when the gift is not exercised at all. Some persons have been ready to imagine they could not pray by the Spirit, but when they exercised the gift of prayer themselves. But this is a great mistake. For though one person be the mouth of the rest to God, yet everyone that joins with him may be justly said to pray in Spirit, if all the graces that are suited to the duty of prayer, and to the expressions that are then used, are found in exercise and lovely vigor. And it is possible that a poor humble Christian may pray in the Spirit, in the secret and silence of his heart, while the person that speaks to God in the name of others hath very little or nothing of the Spirit of God with him, or when the words of the prayer are a known and prescribed form. Though the Spirit of prayer, in the common language of Christians, is never applied to the exercise of the gift where there is no grace, yet it is often applied to the exercise of the grace of prayer without any regard to the gift.

V. FIFTH CAUTION. *Do not expect the same measures of assistance at all times from the Spirit of prayer.* He has nowhere bound himself to be always present with his people, in the same degrees of his influence; though he will never utterly forsake those of whose hearts he has taken possession as his temple and residence. He is compared to the wind, by our Lord Jesus Christ, John 3. The wind blows where and when it listeth, and is not always equal in the strength of its gales, nor constant in blowing on the same part of the earth. The Holy Spirit is a sovereign and free agent, and dispenses his favors in what measure he pleaseth and at what seasons he will.

Those, therefore, that enjoy at present a large share of assistance from the Spirit of prayer should not presume upon it that they shall always enjoy the same. Those that have in any measure lost it should not despair of recovering it again. And those that have not yet been blest with his influences may humbly hope to attain them by seeking. And this naturally leads me to the following section.

Directions to Obtain and Keep the Spirit of Prayer

The last thing I proposed, is to give some *Directions* how to obtain and to keep the assistance of the Holy Spirit; and they are such as these:

DIRECTION 1. *Seek earnestly after converting Grace and Faith in Jesus Christ.* For the Spirit of grace and of supplication dwells in believers only. He may visit others, as he is the author of some spiritual gifts, but he abides only with the saints. The sons of God are so many temples of his Holy Spirit, 1 Cor. 3:16. And he perfumes their souls with the sweet incense of prayer, ascending up from their hearts to God who dwells in heaven. If we are in the flesh, that is, in an unconverted state, we cannot please God, nor walk in the Spirit, nor pray in the Spirit, Rom. 8:9. It is only the children of God that receive his Spirit as a Spirit of adoption, Rom 8:15. "Because ye are sons, he hath sent the Spirit of his Son into your hearts; and it is by faith in Christ Jesus that we receive this Spirit," Gal. 3:14. And wheresoever he is the Spirit of all grace, he will, in some measure, be a Spirit of prayer too.

Let all Christians, therefore, that would maintain and increase in the gifts of the Holy Spirit, live much by the faith of the Son of God, and be frequent in acts of dependance upon

Christ Jesus. For the Spirit is given to him without measure, and in all fullness; that from his fullness we may derive every gift and every grace, John 3:34 and 1:16. As in the natural, so in the spiritual or mystical body, the spirits that give life and activity to the heart and tongue, and to all the members, are derived from the head. He that lives in heaven as our Intercessor and Advocate, to present our addresses and petitions to the throne, will send his own Spirit down to earth to assist us in drawing them up. Live much upon him, therefore, as your Intercessor and your vital Head.

DIRECTION 2. *Give all diligence to acquire this gift, or holy skill, according to the directions concerning the matter, method, and manner of prayer*, which have been laid down before. And be much in the practice of prayer, both in secret and with one another, that young habits may grow, and be improved by exercise. The Spirit of God will come and bless the labors of the mind towards the acquiring of spiritual gifts. Timothy is commanded to give attendance to reading, to meditation on the things of God, and to give himself wholly to the work, that his profiting may appear unto all, though he received gifts of inspiration—1 Tim. 4:3, compared with v. 14, 15, and 2 Tim. 1. And much more should we do it, who are not thus inspired.

Though prophecy was a gift of immediate inspiration, yet there were of old the schools of the prophets, or the college, in which young men were trained up in the study of divine things, that they might be the better prepared to receive the Spirit of prophecy and use and improve it better. And these were called the sons of the prophets, 2 Kings 6:1, 2 Chron. 43:22. St. Paul labored and strove with his natural powers, while the Spirit wrought mightily in him, Col. 1:29.

Do not imagine yourselves to be in danger of quenching the Spirit by endeavoring to furnish yourselves with matter or expression of prayer; for the Spirit of God usually works in and by the use of means. As in the things of nature, so in the things of grace, it is a true and divine proverb, "The soul of the sluggard desireth, and hath not; but the soul of the diligent shall be made fat," Prov. 13:4. We are to put forth our best efforts and then hope for divine assistance; for the Spirit of God helps together with us, Rom. 8:26. As if a man should take hold of one end of a burden in order to raise it, and some mighty helper should make his labor effectual by raising it up at the other end and fulfilling the design. It was the encouragement which David gave his son Solomon, "Arise and be doing and the Lord shall be with thee," 1 Chron. 22:16. While we are stirring up ourselves to obey the command of God and seek his face, we have reason to hope his Spirit will strengthen us to this obedience, and assist us in seeking. As when God commanded Ezekiel to arise and stand upon his feet, and bid him put forth his natural powers towards raising himself, the Spirit entered into him, and set him on his feet, and, by a divine power, made him stand, Ezekiel 2:2.

DIRECTION 3. *Pray earnestly, and pray for the promised Spirit as a Spirit of prayer.* Depend not upon all your natural and acquired abilities, what glorious attainments soever you enjoy. How have some persons been shamefully disappointed, when they have ventured presumptuously to make their addresses to God by the mere strength of their own wit, and memory, and confidence. What hurry and confusion of thought have they fallen into, and been incapable to proceed in the duty! The Holy Spirit shall be given to them that ask aright, Luke, 11:13. Plead the promises of Christ with faith in his name, John 14:16, 17, for he has promised, in his own name, and in his Father's, to send his Holy Spirit.

DIRECTION 4. *Quench not the Spirit of prayer by confining yourselves to any set forms whatsoever.* Though the Spirit of

God may be present and assist in the exercise of grace, while we use forms of prayer, yet let us beware of how we stifle or restrain any holy motions, or good desires and heavenly affections, that are stirred up in our hearts when we pray. If we refuse to express them because we will not vary from the form that is written down before us, we run a great risk of grieving the Holy Spirit and causing him to depart from us, as he is the Spirit of grace; and we effectually hinder ourselves from his assistance in the gift of prayer.

While you borrow the best aids in your devotion from those prayers that are indited by the Spirit of God in Scripture, take care and quench not his farther operations by confining yourselves entirely to those words and expressions. The Holy Spirit may be quenched even by tying yourselves to his own words; for if he had thought those words of Scripture all-sufficient for all the designs and wants of his saints in prayer, he would have given same hint of it in his word. He would have required us to use those prayers always, and there would have been no farther promise of the Spirit to assist us in this work; but now he has promised it, and has forbid us to quench it while we pray without ceasing, 1 Thess. v. 17, 18, 19.

DIRECTION 5. *Dare not to indulge yourselves in a course of spiritual worship in a round of formality and lip-service, without pious dispositions and warm devotion in your own spirits.* There may be danger of this formality and coldness, even in the exercise of the gift of prayer, when we are not tied to a form. And how can we think the Spirit of God will come to our assistance if our spirits withdraw, and are absent from the work?

Take notice of the frame of your minds in prayer; observe the presence or absence of this divine assistant, the Holy Spirit; and since ye are bid to pray always in the Spirit, Eph. 4:18, be not satisfied with any one prayer, where ye have found nothing at all of inward divine yearning towards God through the work of his own Spirit. Oh the dismal character and temper of those souls that pass whole years of worship, and multiply duties and forms of devotion, without end and without number, and no spirit in them!

DIRECTION 6. *Be thankful for every aid of the Spirit of God in prayer, and improve it well.* Spread all the sails of your soul to improve every gale of this heavenly wind that blows when and where it listeth, John 3:8. Comply with his holy yearnings and spiritual motions. Abide in prayer when you feel your graces raised into a lively exercise, "for it is the Spirit that quickeneth," John 6:63. He doth not always come in a sensible manner. Therefore, be tenderly careful lest you shake him off or thrust him from the door of your hearts, especially if he be a rare visitor.

DIRECTION 7. *Beware of pride and self sufficiency, when at any time you feel great enlargements of soul in prayer, and warm affections, and divine delight.* Attribute not to yourselves what is due to God, lest he be provoked. The gift of prayer, in a lively and flowing exercise, will be in danger of puffing up the unwary Christian. But let us remember that it is with the humble that God will dwell, Isa. 57:15, and to the humble he giveth more grace, James 6:6.

DIRECTION 8. *Grieve not the Holy Spirit in the course of your conversation in the world. Walk according to the Spirit, and ye shall not fulfil the lusts of the flesh*, nor make him depart grieved, Eph. 4:29. Hearken to the whispers of the Spirit of God when he convinces of sin, and comply with his secret dictates when he leads to duty, especially the duty of prayer at fit times and seasons. Grieve him not by your unwatchfulness or by wilful sins; resist him not lest he remove; but rather seek greater degrees of his enlightening and sanctifying influences. If you thrust him utterly away from you in the world, he will not take it well at your hands, nor vouchsafe to you his presence in the closet or in the church. If you grieve him before men, he will withdraw from you when you would come near to God, and leave your souls in grief and bitterness. Deal kindly with him, therefore, when he comes to make a visit of conviction to your consciences, and to direct and incline you even to difficult and self-denying duties. Value his presence as a Spirit of knowledge and sanctification, and he will not forsake you as a Spirit of prayer. Live in the Spirit, walk in the Spirit, and then you shall also pray in the Spirit.

Thus have I given short and plain directions how the assistances of the Holy Spirit may be obtained, according to the encouragements of the word of God and the experience of praying Christians. For though he be a sovereign and free agent, and his communications are of pure mercy, so that we can pretend no merit, yet the Spirit of God has so far condescended as to give promises of his own presence to those that seek it in the way prescribed.

I would not finish this section without a word of advice to those from whom the Spirit of prayer is in a great measure withdrawn, in order to their recovering his wonted assistance.

ADVICE 1. *Be deeply sensible of the greatness of your loss; mourn over his absence and lament after the Lord.* Recollect the times when you could pour out your whole heart before God in prayer, with a rich plenty of expressions and lively graces. Compare those shining hours with the dull and dark seasons of retirement which you now complain of. Go and mourn before your God, and say, "How vigorous were all the powers of my nature heretofore in worship! How warm my love! How fervent my zeal! How overflowing was my repentance! And how joyful my thanksgivings and praises! But now, what coldness hath seized my spirit! How dry and dead is my heart, and how far off from God and heaven, even while my knees are bowed before him in secret! How long, O Lord, how long ere thou return again?" Beware of being satisfied with a circle and course of duties without the life, power and pleasure of religion. The Spirit of God will come and revisit the mourners, Jer. 31:20. When God heard Ephraim bemoaning himself, he turned his face towards him with compassion.

ADVICE 2. *Look back and remark the steps whereby the Spirit of God withdrew himself, and search after the sins which provoked him to depart.* He is not wont to go away and leave his saints, except they grieve him.

See if you cannot find some sensual iniquity indulged. He hates this, for he is a Spirit of purity. David might well fear, after his scandalous sin, that God would take away his Holy Spirit from him, Ps. 51:11.

Recollect if you have not rushed upon some presumptuous sin, and run counter to your own light and knowledge: this is a sure way to make him withdraw his favorable presence.

Ask your conscience whether you have not resisted this blessed Spirit, when he hath brought a word of conviction, or command, or reproof to your soul? Whether you have not refused to obey some holy influence, and been heedless of his kind motions in any duty or worship? This highly deserves his resentment and departure.

Reflect whether you have not absented your self sinfully from your closet often, or often left it, almost as soon as you came to it, from a prevailing carnality of mind and sinful weariness of duty; and often shuffled off the work like a tiresome task because you fancied the world called you. It is no wonder then if the Spirit of prayer absent himself from your closet even when the world gives you leave to go thither. And you may expect also, that if you decline secret prayer, the Spirit will not always attend you in public.

Consider whether you have not grown proud and vain in gifts and attainments; and thus the Holy Spirit hath been provoked to leave you to yourself to show you your own weakness and insufficiency, and to abase your pride.

Cry earnestly to him, and beg that he would reveal his own enemy, which hath given him so just offense. And when you have found it out bring it and slay it before the Lord. Confess the sin before him with deep humiliation and self-abasement; abhor, renounce and abandon it forever. Bring it to the cross of Christ for pardon, and there let it be crucified and put to death. Cry daily for strength against it from heaven; renew your engagements to be the Lord's and to walk more watchfully before him.

ADVICE 3. *Remember how you have obtained the Spirit of prayer at first. Read over all the foregoing directions and put them all afresh in practice.*

Was it by faith in Christ Jesus that the Spirit was first received? Then by renewing acts of faith in Christ, seek his return; it is he who first gives, and he who restores this glorious gift.

Was it in the way of labor, duty, and diligence, that you found the Spirit's first assistance? Then stir up all the powers of your soul to the same diligence in duty. And strive and labor to get near to the throne of God, with the utmost exercise of your natural abilities, depending on his secret influences, and hoping for his return. If the wind blow not, labor harder at the oar, and so make your way toward heaven. Dare not indulge a neglect of prayer, upon pretense that the Spirit is departed; for you cannot expect he should revisit you without stirring up your soul to seek him.

Was he given you more sensibly as an answer to prayer at first? Then plead earnestly with God again to restore him. If he furnish you not with matter of prayer by his special and present influences, take with you words from his own holy book, and say to him, "take away all iniquity, and return and receive me graciously," Hos. 14:1, 4. Plead with him his own promises made to returning backsliders, Jer. 3:22; Ezek. 36:25, 31, 37; and put him in mind of the repenting prodigal in the embraces of his father.

When you have found him, hold him fast, and never let him go, Song Sol. 3:4. Dare not again indulge those follies that provoked his anger and absence. Entertain his first appearances with great thankfulness and holy joy. Let him abide with you, and maintain all his sovereignty within you, and see that you abide in him in all subjection. Walk humbly and sin no more, lest a worse thing befall you—lest he depart again from you, and fill your Spirit with fear and bondage, and make you to possess the bitter fruit of your folly; lest he give you up to months and years of darkness, and that measure of the gift of prayer you had attained should be so strangely imprisoned and bound up, that you may be hardly able to pray at all.

COMMENTARY

Seeking Converting Grace

> Seek earnestly after converting Grace and
> Faith in Jesus Christ. For the Spirit of grace
> and of supplication dwells in believers only.
> He may visit others, as He is the author of
> some spiritual gifts, but he abides only with
> the saints. The sons of God are so many
> temples of his Holy Spirit, 1 Cor. 3:16. And he
> perfumes their souls with the sweet incense of
> prayer, ascending up from their hearts to God
> who dwells in heaven. (Page 168)

I was very interested to see this word of counsel in Watts, because the more familiar use of the term "conversion" has to do with a one-time spiritual crisis. It is obvious by its use here that Watts is thinking of it in a way somewhat more similar to the Catholic understanding of conversion as a life-process.

It may be especially helpful to those who have not experienced a crisis-style conversion to look at the Christian journey in this light. Many, if not the majority of Christians, have grown up in "the nurture and admonition of the Lord" with no dramatic experience of a Damascus Road type. It is clear from Christian history that God uses both methods of drawing souls to himself. For some, it means a serious struggle with conviction, a deep and sometimes emotional season of repentance, and the release the soul finds in realizing that it is forgiven and accepted. For others, the soul grows in faith and love for God and for his Son Jesus in the same way the love of parents and others grow. Both are valid and both are the work of grace in the heart.

When Isaac Watts counsels us to "seek earnestly after converting grace and faith in Jesus Christ," he is aware that the spiritual struggle in the soul is real and at times intense. The old nature with which we come into the world hangs on and produces the kind of struggle and confusion Paul talks about in Romans 7: "I have the desire to do what is good, but I cannot carry it out. For what I do is not the good I want to do; no, the evil I do not want to do—this I keep on doing." We all know that the power of temptation is very strong, and we are very weak and inadequate to stand before it without divine assistance.

Prayer for "converting grace and faith in Jesus" is a way of preparing ourselves against these onslaughts. Life is not a smooth road to heaven. It is fraught with many "dangers, toils, and snares." It is a spiritual warfare, whether we like to think of it in those terms or not. If we forget that, we are in greater danger of being led or lured away into spiritual peril.

Watts again comes to our aid with prayer set in the form of hymns. Many of them, of course, are no longer found in our hymn books. The following is from the *Congregational Church Hymnal of England and Wales*, published in the nineteenth century:

> Long have I sat beneath the sound
>   Of thy salvation, Lord;
> But still how weak my faith is found,
>   And knowledge of thy Word!
>
> Oft I frequent thy holy place,
>   And hear almost in vain!
> How small a portion of thy grace
>   My memory can retain!

But cold and feeble is my love!
    How negligent my fear!
How low my hope of joys above!
    How few affections there!

Great God! Thy sovereign power impart,
    To give thy Word success;
Write thy salvation in my heart,
    And make me learn thy grace.

Show my forgetful feet the way
    That leads to joys on high;
There knowledge grows without decay,
    And love shall never die.

One can see how his admonition, "pray for converting grace," fits into the words and thoughts of this hymn. While there is no question that Watts, like others in the Puritan tradition, experienced and expected others to experience a "conversion" which marked the beginning of a conscious change of heart and mind toward God, it is also apparent that such a change had to be nourished by prayer, worship, obedience, repentance, and forgiveness as he continued his spiritual journey.

There has always been a danger of presumption in the "blessed assurance" that banks on a single experience of grace. We do well to heed this admonition as we pursue our own journeys toward our heavenly goal. The words of Watts's hymns often express a healthy self-doubt, and putting these words in the mouths and hearts of those who sang and knew these hymns "by heart" was a way of keeping the Christian from any thought of "cheap grace."

COMMENTARY

This hymn from the *Canadian Methodist Hymn and Tune Book* of 1894 is a prayer for converting grace and faith, a heart-cry to the Holy Spirit for assistance and assurance in our journey:

> Why should the children of a king
>   Go mourning all their days?
> Great Comforter, descend and bring
>   The tokens of thy grace.
>
> Dost thou not dwell in all thy saints,
>   And seal the heirs of heaven?
> When wilt thou banish my complaints,
>   And show my sins forgiven?
>
> Assure my conscience of its part
>   In the Redeemer's blood;
> And bear thy witness with my heart
>   That I am born of God.
>
> Thou art the earnest of his love,
>   The pledge of joys to come;
> May thy blest wings, celestial Dove,
>   Safely convey me home!

A Persuasive to Learn to Pray

CHAPTER FIVE

It is to little purpose that the nature of prayer is explained, that so many rules are framed and directions given to teach persons this divine skill of prayer, if they are not persuaded of the necessity and usefulness of it. I would therefore finish these instructions by leaving some persuasive arguments on the minds of the readers that this attainment is worth their seeking.

I am not going to address myself to those persons who, through a neglect of serious religion, have risen to the insolence of scoffing at all prayers, besides public divine services and authorized forms. Nor am I now seeking to persuade those who may have some taste of serious piety, but, by a superstitious and obstinate veneration of liturgies, have forever abandoned all thoughts of learning to pray.

I think there is enough in the second chapter of this Treatise to convince impartial men that the gift of prayer is no enthusiastical pretense, no insignificant cant of a particular party; but a useful and necessary qualification for all men, a piece of Christian skill to be attained in a rational way by the use of proper means and the blessing of the Holy Spirit. If what I have said can not have influence on these persons, I leave them to the further instruction and reproof of a great and venerable man, whose name I have mentioned before, a learned prelate of the established church, who speaks thus: "For any one to satisfy himself with a form of prayer, is still to remain in infancy. It is the duty of every Christian to grow and increase in all the duties of Christianity, gifts, as well as graces."

Now, how can a man be said to live suitable to these rules, who doth not put forth himself in some attempts and endeavors of this kind? And if it be a fault not to strive and labor after this gift, much more it is to jeer and despise it by the name of extempore prayer, and praying by the Spirit; which expressions (as they are frequently used by some men, by way of reproach) are for the most part a sign of a profane heart, and such as are altogether strangers from the power and comfort of this duty.

My business here is to apply myself to those who have some sense of their obligation to prayer, and of the impossibility of answering all their necessities by any set forms whatever; but, through a coldness and indifference in things of religion, take no pains to acquire the gift, or content themselves with so slight and imperfect a degree of it that themselves or others are not much the better. It is this sort of Christians that I would stir up and awaken to diligence, in seeking so valuable an attainment.

But here I would have it again observed that the qualification I recommend doth not consist in a treasure of sublime notions, florid phrases, and gay eloquence, but merely in a competent supply of religious thoughts, which are the fit materials of prayer, and a readiness to express them in plain and proper words, with a free and natural decency.

1. *The first argument, or persuasive*, I shall draw from the design and dignity of this gift.

There is such a thing as correspondence with heaven, and prayer is a great part of it while we dwell on earth. Who would not be ambitious to correspond with heaven? Who would not be willing to learn to pray? This is the language wherein God hath appointed the sons of Adam, who are but worms and dust, to address the King of Glory, their Maker. And shall there be any among the sons of Adam that will not learn this language? Shall worms and dust refuse this honor and privilege? This is the speech which the sons of God use in talking with their heavenly Father, and shall not all the children know how to speak it? This is the manner and behavior of a saint, and these the expressions of his lips, while his soul is breathing a divine air and stands before God. Why should not every man be acquainted with this manner of address, that he may join in practice with all the saints and have access at all times to the greatest and best of Beings!

There are indeed some sincere Christians who daily worship God, and yet they are often laboring for lack of matter and are perpetually at a loss for proper expressions. They have but a crude attainment of this holy skill. But it is neither their honor nor their interest to perform so divine a work with so many human weaknesses, and yet be satisfied with them. There are children that can but just cry after their Father, and stammer out a broken word or two, by which he can understand their meaning—but these are infants and ungrown.

The Father had rather see his children advancing to manhood, and entertaining themselves daily with that large and free converse with himself which he allows, and to which he graciously invites them.

Prayer is a secret and an appointed mean to obtain all the blessings that we want, whether they relate to this life or the life to come; and shall we not know how to use the means God hath appointed for our own happiness? Shall so glorious a privilege lie unimproved through our neglect?

Were the business of prayer nothing else but to come and beg mercy of God, it would be the duty of every man to know how to draw up such petitions and present them in such a way as becomes a mortal petitioner. But prayer is a work of much larger extent. When a holy soul comes before God, he hath much more to say than merely to beg. He tells his God what a sense he hath of the divine attributes, and what high esteem he pays to his majesty, his wisdom, his power, and his mercy. He talks with him about the works of creation, and stands wrapped up in wonder. He talks about the grace and mystery of redemption, and is yet more filled with admiration and joy. He talks of all the affairs of nature, grace, and glory; he speaks of his works of providence, of love, and vengeance, in this and the future world. Infinite and glorious are the subjects of this holy communion between God and his saints—and shall we content ourselves with sighs and groans, and a few short wishes, and deprive our souls of so rich, so divine, so various a pleasure, for lack of knowing how to furnish out such meditations, and to speak this blessed language!

How excellent and valuable is this *skill of praying*, in comparison of the many lesser arts and accomplishments of human nature that we labor night and day to obtain! What toil do men undergo for seven years together, to acquire the knowledge of a trade and business in this present life! Now the greatest part of the business between us and heaven is transacted in the way of prayer. With how much more diligence should we seek the knowledge of this heavenly commerce than any thing that concerns us merely on earth! How many years of our short life are spent to learn the Greek, the Latin, and the French tongues that we may hold correspondence abroad among the living nations, or converse with the writings of the dead! And shall not the language wherein we converse with heaven, and the living God, be thought worthy equal pains! How nicely do some persons study that art of conversation, that they may be accepted in all company, and share in the favor of men! Is not the same care due to seek all methods of acceptance with God, that we may approve ourselves in his presence? What a high value is set upon human oratory, or the art of persuasion, whereby we are fitted to discourse, and prevail with our fellow-creatures! And is this art of divine oratory of no esteem with us, which teaches us to utter our inward yearnings of the soul, and plead and prevail with our Creator, through the assistance of the Holy Spirit and mediation of our Lord Jesus?

O let the *excellency and high value* of this gift of prayer engage our earnestness and endeavors in proportion to its superior dignity. Let us covet the best of gifts with the warmest desire, and pray for it with ardent supplications, 1 Cor 12:31.

2. *Another argument* may be borrowed from our very character and profession as Christians; some measure of the gift of prayer is of great necessity and universal use to all that are called by the name.

Shall we profess to be followers of Christ, and not know how to speak to the Father? Are we commanded to pray always, and upon all occasions to be constant and fervent in it, and shall we be contented with ignorance and incapacity to obey this command? Are we invited by the warmest exhortations and encouraged by the highest hopes, to draw near to God with all our wants and our sorrows; and shall we not learn to express those wants, and pour out those sorrows before the Lord? Is there a way made for our access to the throne by the blood and intercession of Jesus Christ, and shall we not know how to form a prayer to be sent to heaven and spread before the throne, by this glorious intercession! Is his Holy Spirit promised to teach us to pray, and shall a Christian be careless or unwilling to receive such divine teachings?

There is not any faculty in the whole Christian life that is called out into so frequent exercise as this. And it is a most unhappy thing to be always at a loss to perform the work which daily necessity requires and daily duty demands. Will a person profess to be a scholar that cannot read? Shall any man pretend to be a minister that can not preach? And it is but a poor pretense we make to Christianity, if we are not able, at least in secret, to supply ourselves with a few meditations, or expressions, to continue a little in this work of prayer.

Remember, then, O Christian, this is not a gift that belongs to ministers alone, nor alone to governors of families, who are under constant obligation to pray in public, though it most highly concerns them to be expert in this holy skill, that with courage and presence of mind, with honor and decency, they may discharge this part of their duty to God in their congregations and households. But this duty hath a farther extent. Every man that is joined to a church of Christ should seek after an ability to help the church with his prayers; or at least, upon more private occasions, to join with a few fellow-Christians in seeking to God their Father. Nor are women, though they are forbidden to speak in the church, forbid to pray in their own families, nor with one another in a private chamber. And I am persuaded that Christians would ask one another's assistance more frequently in prayer upon special occasions, if a good gift of prayer were more commonly sought and more universally obtained. Nor would congregations in the country be dismissed, and the whole Lord's day pass without public worship, where a minister is suddenly taken sick, if some grave and discreet Christian, of good ability in prayer, would but take that part of worship upon him, together with the reading of some well composed sermon, and some useful portion of Holy Scripture. Doubtless this would be most acceptable to that God who loves the gates of Zion, or his own public ordinances, more than all the dwellings of Jacob, or worship of private families, Ps. 87:2.

Thus far is this gift necessary, wheresoever social prayer may be performed. But the necessity of it reaches farther still. There is not a man, woman or child that is capable of seeking God, but is bound to exercise something of the gift of prayer. And those that never have any call from Providence to be the mouth of others in speaking to God, are called daily to speak to God themselves. It is necessary, therefore, that every soul should be so far furnished with a knowledge of the perfections of God, as to be able to adore them distinctly; should have such an acquaintance with its own needs, as to express them particularly before God, at least in the conceptions and language of the mind; should have such a grasp of the encouragement to pray, as to be able to plead with God for supply; and should have such an observation and remembrance of divine mercies, as to repeat some of them before God, with humble thanksgivings.

3. I would pursue this persuasive by a *third argument*, drawn from the divine delight, and exceeding great advantage of this gift to our own souls, and to the souls of all that join in prayer with us.

Christians, have you never felt your spirits raised from a carnal and vain temper of mind to a devout frame, by a lively fervency of prayer? Have you not found your whole souls overspread with holy affections and carried up to heaven with most abundant pleasure, by the pious and regular performance of him that speaks to God in worship? And when ye have been cold and indifferent to divine things, have ye not felt that heavy and listless humor expelled, by joining with the warm and lively expressions of a person skillful in his duty? How sweet a refreshment have ye found under inward burdens of mind, or outward afflictions, when in broken language you have told them to your minister, and he hath spread them before God, and that in such words as have spoken your whole soul and your sorrows! And you have experienced a sweet serenity and calmness of spirit; you have risen up from your knees with your countenance no more sad. And have you not wished for the same gift yourselves, that you might be able, upon all occasions, thus to address the throne of grace, and pour out all your hearts in this manner before your God? But what a sad inconvenience is it to live in such a world as this, where we are liable daily to so many new troubles and temptations, and not be able to express them to God in prayer unless we find them written in the words of a form; and how hard it is to find any form suited to all our new wants and new sorrows!

At other times, what divine impressions of holiness have ye felt in public worship in the congregation where this duty hath been performed with holy skill and fervency! And in that prayer you have received more solid edification than from the whole sermon. How dead have you been to all sinful temptations, and how much devoted to God. And do ye not long to be able to pray thus in your households, and in your own closets? Would it not be a pleasure for men to be thus able to entertain their whole families daily; and for Christians thus to entertain one another, when they meet to pray to their common God and Father, and to help one another at this rate, onward to the world of praise! When the disciples had just been witnesses of the devotion of our Lord, Luke 11:1, who spake as never man spake, their hearts grew warm under the words of that blessed worshiper; and one of them, in the name of the rest, cried out, "Lord, teach us to pray," too.

Thus, a good attainment of this gift is made a happy instrument of sanctification as well as comfort, by the co-working power of the blessed Spirit.

But on the other hand, hath not your painful experience sometimes taught you that zeal and devotion have been cooled, and almost quenched, by the vain repetitions or weak and wandering thoughts of some fellow-Christian that leads the worship? And at another time, a well-framed prayer, of beautiful order and language, hath been rendered disagreeable by some unhappy tones and gestures; so that you have been ready to long for the conclusion, and have been weary of attendance.

Who then would willingly remain ignorant of such an attainment, which is so sweet and successful an instrument to advance religion, in the powers and pleasures of it in their own hearts, and the hearts of all men that are around about them!

4. *The honor of God, and the credit of religion, in the world*, will afford me another spring of arguments, to excite you to attain this skill of prayer.

The great God esteems himself dishonored when we do not pay him the best worship we are capable of. The work of the Lord must not be done negligently. It is highly for his honor that we be furnished with the best talents for his service, and that we employ them in the best manner. This reveals to the world the inward high esteem and veneration we have for our Maker. This gives him glory in the eyes of men. But to neglect utterly this gift of prayer, and to serve him daily with only a few sudden thoughts, with rude and improper expressions that never cost us any thing but the labor of our lips while we speak—this is not the way to sanctify his name among men.

There is a sinful sloth and indifference in religion that hath tempted some men to believe that God is no curious and exact inquirer into outward things. And if they can but persuade themselves their intentions are right, they imagine that for the substance and form of their sacrifice anything will serve. And, as though he were not a God of order, they address him often in confusion. Because the heart is the chief thing in divine worship, (like some foolish Israelites) they are regardless what beast they offer him, so it hath but a heart. But the prophet Malachi thunders with divine indignation and jealousy against such worshipers. "Ye have brought that which was torn and lame and the sick: Should I accept this at your hand? I am a great King, saith the Lord of Hosts, and my name is dreadful," Mal.1:13, 14. He upbraids us with sharp resentment and bids us offer it to our Governor, and asks if he will be pleased with it. Now, our consciences sufficiently inform us how careful we are when we make an address to an earthly Governor to have our thoughts well ordered, and words well chosen, as well as to tender it with a loyal heart. And may not our supreme Governor in heaven expect a due care in ordering our thoughts and choosing our words, so far at least as to answer all the designs of prayer; and so far as is consistent with the necessity of so frequent addresses to him and our other Christian duties!

The credit of religion in the world is much concerned in the honorable discharge of the duty of prayer.

There is an inward beauty in divine worship that consists in the devout temper of the worshipers, and the lively exercise of holy affections; but of this God only is witness, who sees the heart. There is also an outward beauty that arises from a decent and acceptable performance of all the parts of it that come within the notice of our fellow-creatures; that those who observe us may be forced to acknowledge the excellence of religion in our practice of it.

Where worship is performed by immediate inspiration, a natural order of things and a becoming behavior are required in him especially who leads the worship. This is the design of the apostle in his advice to the Corinthians: "Let all things be done decently and in order," 1 Cor. 14:40; i.e., Let such a prudent conduct, such a regular and rational management, in all the parts of worship be found among you, as gives a natural beauty to human actions, and will give a visible glory to the acts of religion. Where this advice is followed, if the unlearned and unbeliever, (i.e, ignorant and profane,) come into the assembly, they will fall down and worship God, and report, God is in you of a truth, ver. 25. But if you are guilty of disorder of speaking, and break the rules of natural light and reason in uttering your inspirations, the unlearned and unbelievers will say you are mad, though your words may be the dictates of the Holy Spirit.

Much more is this applicable to our common and ordinary performance of worship. When an unskillful person speaks in prayer with a heaviness and penury of thought, with crude and improper language, with a false and offensive tone of voice, or accompanies his words with awkward motions, what slanders are thrown upon our practice! A whole party of Christians is ridiculed, and the scoffer saith we are mad. But when a minister, or master of a family, with a fluency of devout sentiments and language offers his petitions and praises to God in the name of all that are present, and observes all the rules of natural decency in his voice and gesture, how much credit is done to our profession hereby, even in the opinion of those who have no kindness for our way of worship. And how effectually doth such a performance confute the pretended necessity of imposing forms. How gloriously doth it triumph over the slanders of the adversary, and force a conviction upon the mind, that there is something divine and heavenly among us!

I cannot represent this in a better manner than it is done by an ingenious author of the last age; who, being a courtier in the reigns of the two brothers, Charles and James II, can never lie under the suspicion of being a dissenter; and that is the late Marquis of Halifax. This noble writer, in a little book, under a borrowed character, gives his own sentiments of things. He tells us that:

> He is far from relishing the impertinent wanderings of those who pour out long prayers upon the congregation, and all from their own stock; a barren soil, which produces weeds instead of flowers; and by this mean they expose religion itself, rather than promote men's devotions. On the other side, there may be too great restraint put upon men, whom God and nature have distinguished from their fellow-laborers, by blessing them with a happier talent, and by giving them not

only good sense, but a powerful utterance too, has enabled them to gush out upon the attentive auditory, with a mighty stream of devout and unaffected eloquence. When a man so qualified, endued with learning too, and, above all, adorned with a good life, breaks out into a warm and well delivered prayer before his sermon, it has the appearance of a divine rapture; he raises and leads the hearts of the assembly in another manner than the most composed, or best studied form of set words can do. And the pray we's, who serve up all their sermons with the same garnishing, would look like so many statues, or men of straw, in the pulpit, compared with those that speak with such a powerful zeal, that men are tempted at the moment, to believe heaven itself has dictated their words to them.

5. A *fifth persuasive* to seek the gift of prayer shall be drawn from the easiness of obtaining it, with the common assistance of the Holy Spirit. Easy, I call it, in comparison of the long toil and difficulty that men go through in order to acquire a common knowledge in arts, sciences, or trades in this world; though it is not to be expected without some pains and diligence.

Some young persons may be so foolish and unhappy as to make two or three bold attempts to pray in company before they have well learned to pray in secret; and finding themselves much at a loss and bewildered in their thoughts, or confounded for want of presence of mind, they have abandoned all hopes, and contented themselves with saying it is impossible. And as they have tempted God by rashly venturing upon such an act of worship, without any due care and preparation, so they have afterward thrown the blame of their own sloth upon God himself, and cried, "It is a mere gift of heaven, but God hath not bestowed it upon me." This is as if a youth who had just begun to read logic should attempt immediately to dispute in a public school, and finding himself baffled and confounded, should cast away his book, renounce his studies, and say, "I shall never learn it, it is impossible": whereas, when we seek any attainment, we must begin both regularly and gradually toward perfection, with patience and labor. Let but the rules recommended in the second chapter of this Treatise for acquiring the gift of prayer be duly followed, and I doubt not but a Christian of ordinary capacity may, in time, gain so much of this skill as to answer the demands of his duty and his station.

Rather than I would be utterly destitute of this gift of prayer, I would make such an experiment as this: Once a month I would draw up a new prayer for myself in writing, for morning and evening, and for the Lord's day, according to all parts of this duty prescribed in the first chapter of this book, or out of the Scriptures that Mr. Menry hath collected in his Method of Prayer, (which book I would recommend to all Christians). I would use it constantly all that month; yet never confining myself all along to those very same words, but giving myself a liberty to put in, or leave out, or enlarge, according to the present workings of my heart or occurrences of providence. Thus by degrees I would write less and less, at last setting down little more than headings or hints of thought, or expression—just as ministers learn by degrees to leave off their sermon-notes in preaching. I would try whether a year or two of this practice would not furnish me with an ability, in some measure, to pray without this help, always making it one of my petitions that God would pour more of his Spirit upon me and teach me the skill of praying. And by such short abstracts and general headings of prayer, well drawn up for children, according to their years and knowledge, they may be taught to pray by degrees, and begin before they are six years old.

OBJECTION. If any Christian that loves his ease should abuse this proposal and say, "If I may use this prayer of my own framing for a month together, why may I not use it all my life, and so give myself no farther trouble about learning to pray?"

ANSWER 1. I would first desire such a man to read over again the great inconveniencies mentioned in the second chapter, that arise from a perpetual use of forms, and the danger of confinement to them.

ANSWER 2. I would say in the second place, the matter of prayer is almost infinite; it extends to everything we can have to transact with our Maker; and it is impossible, in a few pages, to mention particularly, one tenth part of the subjects of our converse with God. But in drawing up new prayers every month, in time, we may run through a great part of those subjects, and grow, by degrees, to be habitually furnished for converse with him on all occasions whatsoever; which can never be done by dwelling always upon one form or two. As children that learn to read at school daily take out new lessons, that they may be able at last to read everything; which they would not well attain if they always dwelt on the same lesson.

ANSWER 3. Besides, there is a blessed variety of expressions in Scripture to represent our wants, sorrows, and dangers; the glory, power, and grace of God; his promises and covenant; our hopes and discouragements. And sometimes one expression, sometimes another, may best suit our present turn of thought and temper of our minds. It is good, therefore, to have as large a furniture of this kind as possible, that we might never be at a loss to express the inward sentiments of our soul, and clothe our desires and wishes in such words as are most exactly fitted to them.

ANSWER 4. Though God is not the more affected with variety of words and arguments in prayer, (for he acts upon other principles borrowed from himself,) yet our natures are more affected with such a variety. Our graces are drawn into more vigorous exercise, and, by our importunity in pleading with God, with many arguments, we put ourselves more directly under the promise that is made to importunate petitioners; and we become fitter to receive the mercies we seek.

Yet in the last place, I would answer by way of confession: If we have the scheme and substance of several prayers ready composed, and well suited to all the most usual cases and concerns of life and religion, and if one or other of these be daily used with seriousness, interposing new expressions wherever the soul is drawn out to further the yearnings after God, or where it finds occasion for new matter from some present providence—this is much rather to be approved than a neglect of all prayer, or a dwelling upon a single form or two; and it will be more edifying to those who join with us, than a perpetual confusion of thought and endless dishonorable attempts in the mere extemporary way.

But I speak this by way of indulgence to persons of weaker gifts, or when the natural spirits are low, or the mind much indisposed for duty. And in these cases the way of addressing God which is called mixed prayer will be so far from confining the pious soul to a dread form of worship, that it will sometimes prove a sweet enlargement and release to the spirit under its own darkness and confinement. It will furnish it with spiritual matter, and awaken it to a longer and more lively converse with God in its own language. And, if I may use a plain comparison, it will be like pouring a little water into a pump, whereby a much greater quantity will be raised from the spring when it lies low in the earth.

OBJECTION. If any Christian, on the other hand, should forbid all use of such compositions, as supposing them utterly unlawful and quenching the Spirit.

ANSWER. I would humbly reply, there is no danger of that while we do not rest in them as our designed end, but use them only as means to help us to pray, and never once confine ourselves to them without the liberty of alteration.

It is the saying of a great divine; "Though set forms made by others be as a crutch, or help of our insufficiency, yet those which we compose ourselves, are fruits of our sufficiency: and that while a man ought not to be so confined by any premeditated form, as to neglect any special infusion, he ought so to prepare himself, as if he expected no assistance: and he should so depend upon divine assistance, as if he had made no preparation."

Here, if I might obtain leave of my fathers in the ministry, I would say this to younger students, that if in their private years of study they pursued such a course, once a week, as I have here described, I am persuaded their gifts would be richly improved; their ministerial labors would be universally acceptable to the world; their talents would be more attractive of multitudes to their place of worship; the hearers would be raised in their spirits, while the preacher prays with a regular and divine eloquence: and they would receive those sermons with double influence and success, which are attended with such prayers.

6. The last attempt I shall make to convince Christians of the necessity of seeking this gift, shall be merely by representing the ill consequences of the neglect of it. If you take no pains to learn to pray, you will unavoidably fall into one of these three evils:

Either, first, you will drag on heavily in the work of prayer all your days, even in your closets as well as your family, and be liable to so many imperfections in the performance as will rob your own soul of a great part of the benefit and the delight of this sweet duty, and give neither pleasure nor profit to them that hear you. The ignorant part of your household will sleep under you, while the more knowing are in pain for you. And perhaps you will sometimes think to make amends for the dullness of the devotion by increasing the length of it; but this is to add one error to another, and lay more burdens upon them that are weary.

Or, secondly, if you find that you cannot carry on the constancy of this duty with tolerable satisfaction, you will give yourself up to a morning and evening form, and rest in them from year to year. Now, though it may be possible for some persons to use a form without deadness, and formality of spirit; yet such as, from a mere principle of sloth, neglect to learn to pray, are most likely to fall into formality and slothfulness in the use of forms; and the power of religion will be lost.

Or, in the last place, if you have been bred up with an universal hatred to all forms of prayer, and yet know how to pray without them, you will first grow inconstant in the discharge of this duty. Every little hindrance will put you by; and at last, perhaps, you will leave it off entirely; and your house and your closet too, in time, will be without prayer.

Christians, which of these three evils will ye choose? Can you be satisfied to drudge on to your life's end among improprieties and indecencies, and thus expose prayer to contempt? Or will your minds be easy to be confined forever, to a form or two of slothful devotion? Or shall prayer be banished out of your houses, and all appearance of religion be lost among you?

Parents, which of these evils do ye choose for your children? You charge them to pray; daily you tell them the sin and danger of dwelling all upon prayer books, and yet you scarce ever give them any regular instructions how to perform this duty. How can ye expect they should maintain religion honorably in their families, and avoid the things you forbid? But whatsoever ill consequences attend them hereafter, consider what share of the guilt will lie at the door of those who never took any pains to show them to pray!

While I am persuading Christians with so much earnestness to seek the gift of prayer, surely none will be so weak as to imagine the grace and Spirit of prayer may be neglected. Without some degrees of common influence from the blessed Spirit, the gift is not to be attained: and without the exercise of grace in this duty, the prayer will never reach heaven nor prevail with God. He is not taken with the brightest forms of worship, if the heart be not there. Be the thoughts ever so divine, the expressions ever so sprightly, and delivered with all the sweet and moving accents of speech, it is all in his esteem but a fair outer shell without a soul. It is a mere picture of prayer, a dead picture, which cannot charm; a lifeless offering, which the living God will never accept; nor will our great High Priest ever present it to the Father.

But these things do not fall directly under my present design. I would therefore recommend my readers to those treatises that enforce the necessity of spiritual worship, and describe the glory of inward devotion above the best outward performances. Then shall they learn the perfection of beauty in this part of worship, when the gift and grace of prayer are happily joined, in the secret pleasure and success of it, and appear before men in its full loveliness and attractive power. Then shall religion look like itself, divine and heavenly, and shine in all the lustre it is capable of here upon earth.

The Glory of Inward Devotion

"I would therefore recommend my readers to those treatises that enforce the necessity of spiritual worship, and describe the glory of inward devotion. . . ." (Page 200)

Watts did not intend this book for those who were advanced in the life of prayer. He designed it especially for "young Christians"—those who are beginners in the exciting and challenging opportunity of prayer. Much of the book is obviously aimed at correcting unhappy and unfortunate ways of praying that interfere with a spirit of worship and draw attention to the person who is praying. The faults that Isaac Watts addressed in the early eighteenth century are still with us today. Extempore prayer is too often *self-conscious prayer.* Resorting to prayers read from a book is acceptable in some situations, but does not work when praying in and with a group. Then the need to forget oneself and "pray in the Spirit" is paramount.

Real prayer can grow only out of inward devotion. It is this state of mind and heart that makes prayer a constant source of strength and hope. If we listen to those who have ventured farther down this road, they tell us that such inward devotion can be obtained. They also assure us that it is immanently worthwhile.

In one of his hymns, Watts helps believers to express our utter dependence upon God and the great privilege that is ours because of his grace. Here again, he helps us more by the words he gives us to express our heart's desire than by any arguments about our need for inward devotion.

My God, my life, my love,
To Thee, to Thee I call;
I cannot live if thou remove,
For thou art all in all.

To thee, and thee alone,
The angels owe their bliss;
They sit around thy gracious throne,
And dwell where Jesus is.

Not all the harps above
Can make a heavenly place,
If God his residence remove,
Or but conceal his face.

Nor earth, nor all the sky
Can one delight afford,
No, not a drop of real joy
Without thy presence, Lord.

Thou art the sea of love,
Where all my pleasures roll,
The circle where my passions move,
And center of my soul.

Theophan the Recluse was a spiritual master of the Russian Church in the nineteenth century. These spiritual counselors of the Orthodox Church have made much of the need for continual prayer. Theophan says:

"Pray without ceasing," St. Paul writes to the Thessalonians (I Thess. 5:17). And in other epistles, he commands, "Praying always with all supplication in the spirit" (Eph. 6:18). . . . It is clear from this that unceasing prayer is not an accidental prescription, but the essential characteristic of the Christian spirit. The life of a Christian, according to the Apostle, "is hid with Christ in God" (Col. 3:3). So the Christian must live in God continuously, with attention and feeling: to do this is to pray without ceasing. . . .

It is clear to everyone that the advice of the Apostle is not carried out merely by the practice of established prayers at certain set hours, but requires a permanent walking before God, a dedication of all one's activities to Him who is all-seeing and omnipresent, an ever-fervent appeal to heaven with the mind and heart. The whole of life, in all its manifestations, must be permeated by prayer. But its secret is love for the Lord. . . .[1]

Do we truly know the glory of inward devotion or the necessity of maintaining it if we are to walk with God? In his *Confessions*, St. Augustine, writing in the early fifth century, has come face to face with his own past failure to recognize and relate to God. The entire book is an account of his pilgrimage toward his spiritual home in the bosom of the Church. He addresses God in words that would be appropriate for many of us who have often neglected the practice of God's presence:

Too late have I loved you, O Beauty, ancient yet ever new. Too late have I loved you! And behold, you were within, but I was outside, searching for you there—plunging, deformed amid those fair forms which you had made. You were with me, but I was not with you. Things held me far from you, which, unless they were in you did not exist at all. You called and shouted, and burst my deafness. You breathed fragrant odors on me, and I held back my breath, but now I pant for you. I tasted, and now I hunger and thirst for you. You touched me, and now I yearn for your peace.[2]

Watts's morning hymn that follows expresses a perpetual awareness of God's presence and mercies. Each new day brings these mercies to mind, and each evening we rest in the assurance of their continuance. Watts's final lines echo a thought similar to the more familiar one, "Love so amazing, so divine, demands my soul, my life, my all."

> My God, how endless is thy love!
> Thy gifts are every evening new;
> And morning mercies from above
> Gently distill like early dew.
>
> Thou spread'st the curtains of the night,
> Great Guardian of my sleeping hours;
> Thy sovereign word restores the light,
> And quickens all my drowsy powers.
>
> I yield my powers to thy command,
> To thee I consecrate my days;
> Perpetual blessings from thy hand
> Demand perpetual songs of praise.

"The glory of inward devotion" is a gift that God offers to us all. Isaac Watts has rightly set the reality of this relationship with God above all forms and methods of prayer. And as the journey of a thousand miles begins with one footstep, so our progress in this inward devotion must begin where we are, with the small steps of beginners who have tasted and have begun to see that the Lord is gracious.

---

[1] *The Art of Prayer* (London: Faber and Faber), pp. 81, 82.
[2] *The Confessions of St. Augustine*, Hal M. Helms, ed. (Paraclete Press, Brewster MA, 1986), 210-211.